GOING BEYOND

STUDY GUIDE

RAY PETTY

FROM YOUR PATH OF DISAPPOINTMENT TO GOD'S OVERCOMING LOVE

THIRTEEN LESSONS FOR INDIVIDUAL OR GROUP STUDY

Melbourne, Florida USA

GOING BEYOND—From Your Path of Disappointment to God's Overcoming Love
by Ray Petty

Parsons Publishing House
P. O. Box 410063
Melbourne, FL 32941 USA
www.ParsonsPublishingHouse.com
Info@ParsonsPublishingHouse.com

Publisher's Note: Publisher has opted to reference satan and related names with lowercase letters.

ISBN-13: 978-1602731059
ISBN-10: 1602731055
Library of Congress Control Number: 2019932329
Printed in the United States of America.
For World-Wide Distribution.

WHAT ARE PEOPLE SAYING?

Are you spiritually stuck because of things that have happened or are happening to you? Do you need to get beyond these things? Do you believe that God wants to take you to another level in your spiritual life beyond where you have ever been or even imagined? Ray Petty's book can help you do that—individually or as a group. I recommend it to you.

—Rev. Dr. Frank H. Billman
Founder of the Methodist School for Supernatural Ministry and Supernatural Ministry Intensives; Adjunct Professor and DMin Mentor for the Doctor of Ministry in Supernatural Ministry at United Theological Seminary; Scholar in Residence for the Methodist Church of Barbados
Nashville, Tennessee USA

In an age where the Church is crippled by misleading red letter Christianity, Ray Petty takes the whole Biblical Testament seriously. Suffering and struggle are normal for the Jesus follower, and this book will help you discover the narrative wisdom to see you through to hope and peace.

—Rev. Dr. Jay Ferguson
Senior Pastor, First UMC Bluefield
Bluefield, Virginia USA

Many of us stop growing spiritually and settle for something less than God's full desire for our lives. In his latest book, Ray Petty helps us identify some of the barriers and strongholds in our way, then gives guidance on how to turn these stumbling blocks into stepping stones that will draw us into God's purpose for our lives. By seeing examples of real-life people from the Old and New Testaments, you will come away motivated to pursue God's unique destiny for you.

Pastor Ray's insights from Scripture, "Pivot Points," guided prayer, and discussion questions in each lesson all help to activate the power of these truths in your own life.

—Rev. Doug Wilder
Pastor, Ebenezer and Chestnut UMC
Knoxville, Tennessee USA

TABLE OF CONTENTS

Lesson 1

INTRODUCTION

⌘

The phrase "going beyond" began stirring in my spirit as I was about to step into one of the greatest discoveries the Lord has ever opened to me. The phrase "going beyond" reminds me of those places where I stopped short of God's best and His purpose for my life. Yet, at the same time, I felt an excitement—a sense of hope rising within me—that God was about to do something wonderful and liberating in those places, times, events, and yes, even setbacks where I stopped short of a new level of victorious living.

Going beyond is when the seeds of doubt, failure, and disappointment begin falling away, and they are replaced with the joy of knowing that breakthrough is coming and that God is restoring what the enemy has stolen. We start to receive a fresh measure of God's grace pouring into our lives, and He takes us to a place called "Beyond." Joseph experiences this when his brothers sell him into slavery, but God means it for good (Genesis 50:20).

The word "beyond" can be defined as *not stopping short of God's plan, purpose, destiny, and His best for our lives.* It is when the enemy intends something for evil, God brings forth something powerful, and even better.

I came across this phrase "going beyond" while reading ***Time to Defeat the Devil*** by Chuck Pierce. He said, "There is a place called 'Beyond' that the Lord is calling you to. See your place called 'Beyond' and start pressing toward that place!"[1] This has become God's Word to me that stirs my spirit to pursue that place called "beyond" the defeats, frustrations, and setbacks, to a revelation of God's goodness, grace, and power to restore, to heal, and to redeem what the enemy means for evil.

Something radical happens in our thinking and in our spirit when we declare before the Lord: "*Take me beyond my last defeat. Take me beyond the last place where I fell short. Take me beyond the last negative word I spoke over my life or the last negative word spoken against me. Take me beyond defeat to victory.*" When we begin to pray this way, something shifts, and we begin to think differently, believe differently, and live differently.

I found myself repenting (changing my mind and my believing), and began declaring that my best days are ahead of me and that the Father is taking me where I cannot go on my own. I have discovered a grace working in my life that reveals Jesus as the Overcomer who lives in me and enables me to be an overcomer. I have repented for the times I stop short or fail to go beyond the tests, difficulties, and challenges. I repent for my lack of faith to believe that God could provide a breakthrough in all of those instances.

Going beyond is my prayer each day: "Father, I thank you that Your Holy Spirit is strengthening me in my inner man to go beyond where I have stopped short of experiencing Your glory." As a pastor, God was taking me beyond where

I stopped short in fulfilling His purpose and plan. He was taking me beyond the hurtful, discouraging words of others where I could declare, "*Father, take me beyond every discouraging thought the enemy has planted in my mind. Father, take me beyond every hurtful and discouraging word, to speak words of forgiveness, releasing, and blessing.*"

The key to going beyond is looking to Jesus past the defeats, past the wrong choices, and past the hurtful words. By fixing your eyes on Him and in the light of His presence, He takes us beyond where we cannot go on our own.

When we receive this revelation about going beyond, we discover more about the nature and character of God. He desires to take us beyond our failures, to move past frustrations, disappointments, and setbacks, so we come to grips with the truth that God is good and desires good for our lives. When we have this realization, we display His glory (2 Corinthians 4:6).

When I release my fears so that God could take me beyond those places and instances where I did not finish well, God comes and says, "*Let Me take you beyond your fear, your defeat, your anger, your setbacks, and your frustration to a place called Beyond.*" There I find an abundance of God's grace as He gives me new eyes through which to see things, people, and events. God's leading allows me to triumph through Christ. Going beyond releases the fragrance of His presence and His goodness.

My prayer is that through this book we will discover God's prophetic Word, and we will go beyond where you thought you could ever go. Turn your eyes toward Jesus to see past all the stuff and see Him taking you to a place called "Beyond."

Destined for Greatness

Destiny is a choice to live from God's best, His highest purpose, and His calling. We can miss our destiny by demanding our way over God's way because destiny is living from God's best and receiving all that He says we can have and become. When we step into our future, we also release our destiny which is to become like Christ (2 Corinthians 3:18). We step into our destiny when we desire God's best, His purpose, and His calling. We release our destiny to the degree that we are willing to step into God's best. **Walking in fear and listening to the lies of the enemy are two major factors that keep us from stepping into God's best.**

Our destiny is receiving God's best, His purpose, and calling upon our lives as we are conformed to the image of Christ. This means we are not living **for** it, as if it is something to be achieved, but we are living **from** our destiny, for our "life is hidden with Christ in God" (Colossians 3:3). Our destiny has already been achieved for us through Christ. We are living **from** the Kingdom of God for His Kingdom is within us, and this is why we can live **from** our destiny, not **for** our destiny.

When we do not believe we are destined for greatness, we will always live below God's best, His highest desire, and His calling. Greatness comes not from accomplishments, pedigree, importance, or fame, but from receiving God's grace working in our lives.

If we make greatness our ambition, **we are responsible** for making something out of ourselves. But when we make God's grace the desire and ambition of the heart, then **He is responsible** for creating something out of us that is uniquely ours.

We have been destined for greatness not from the applause of men, but from the applause of heaven. The Bible states that God looks at the heart while men look at the outward appearance (1 Samuel 16:7). God deposits in the creation of mankind His very nature so that the heart of man desires something great and wonderful "that through these [great and precious promises] you may be partakers of the divine nature" (2 Peter 1:4b). The Psalmist speaks of the wonder of creation and how God has created us for greatness:

> For You formed my inward parts; You covered me in my mother's womb. I will praise You, for I am fearfully and wonderfully made; marvelous are Your works, and that my soul knows very well (Psalms 139:13-14).

We are fearfully and wonderfully made, created in the image of God, and have been called into a dynamic relationship with Jesus Christ. God wants us to know: we are not accidents, we have not been given lesser gifts or abilities, and His thoughts toward us are precious. We have been destined for greatness—destined to rule and reign with Christ. Paul declares that Christ has "raised us up together, and made us sit together in the heavenly places in Christ Jesus" (Ephesians 2:6) so that we are destined to be overcomers in this life.

Sometimes fear keeps us from stepping into the greatness for which God has created us because of what others have said about us or what we have believed about ourselves. The Psalmist says our greatness is not from human ingenuity, but God's grace is working in us for why we have been created. Paul says it this way:

> For consider your calling, brothers: not many of you were wise according to worldly standards, not many were powerful, not many were of noble birth. But God chose what is foolish in the world to shame the wise; God chose what is weak in the world to shame the strong; God chose what is low and despised in the world, even things that are not, to bring to nothing things that are, so that no human being might boast in the presence of God. And because of him you are in Christ Jesus, who became to us wisdom from God, righteousness and sanctification and redemption, so that, as it is written, "Let the one who boasts, boast in the Lord (1 Corinthians 1:26-31, ESV).

God uses our very weakness to bring glory and honor to Him. It is the greatness of His power working in us that empowers us for a life destined for greatness. Paul's prayer for the church at Ephesus is that they grasp—understand—what riches we have in knowing Christ Jesus: "And what is the exceeding **greatness of His power** toward us who believe, according to the working of His mighty power" (Ephesians 1:19, emphasis added). The reason we can live from our destiny of greatness is because of the greatness of God's power working in us. We are able to achieve only what God is able to do in us and through us, and that is absolutely amazing! Greatness is not dependent upon our greatness, but upon God's greatness working in us. It is about God's grace being poured out in us and through us. Any great thing we do is because of the lavish greatness of God in our lives.

Stepping into greatness is to know who we are in Jesus Christ as sons and daughters. It is in the small things of serving the Lord where we are while allowing the Lord to use us and to demonstrate His goodness and His greatness. It is not the great thing we do that makes it great, but the surrendering of ourselves to His Lordship, and He does something extraordinary through us.

Sometimes we are too intimidated to step into our destiny of greatness because of what we have said, done, or thought. We feel it might disqualify us from greatness. This is satan's lie to keep us from our destiny: "The thief's purpose is to steal and kill and destroy" (John 10:10a, NLT), or we hesitate because our thoughts have not been brought captive to the obedience of Christ (2 Corinthians 10:4-5). The enemy does not want us to step into the knowledge that we are destined for greatness, but to keep you thinking and believing smaller than we are intended to think or believe. We are destined for greatness because the Father has begun a mighty work in us, and He brings us to a place of strength and maturity (Philippians 1:6).

We might ask the question: how and in what way are we destined for greatness? Peter writes, "Therefore humble yourselves under the mighty hand of God, that He may exalt you in due time" (1 Peter 5:6). **The way to greatness is the way of brokenness and humility.** The way to greatness is staying connected to Jesus, the Vine, and learning to become overcomers. In the eyes of the Lord, we are great, "for we are His workmanship, created in Christ Jesus for good works...that we should walk in them" (Ephesians 2:10). We are God's creation, and He has uniquely placed His gifts in us and upon us to display His glory. The Father's authority rests upon us so that we can do those things that we were created to do.

Can anything ever separate us from Christ's love? Does it mean He no longer loves us if we have trouble or calamity, or we are persecuted, hungry, destitute, in danger, or threatened with death?

> (As the Scripture say, "For your sake we are killed every day; we are being slaughtered like sheep.") No, despite all these things, overwhelming victory is ours through Christ, who loved us. And I am convinced that nothing can ever separate us from God's love. Neither death nor life, neither angels nor demons, neither our fears for today nor our worries about tomorrow—not even the powers of hell can separate us from God's love. No power in the sky above or in the earth below—indeed, nothing in all creation will ever be able to separate us from the love of God that is revealed in Christ Jesus our Lord (Romans 8:36-39, NLT).

This book is for all who have struggled to come into their rightful place as God's sons and daughters; for all who have not known how to relate to Papa, *Abba* Father; for all who have lived under the tyranny of intimidation, fear, and defeat; and who have longed to experience Christ's

freedom, His amazing love, and His absolute acceptance. This book is for those who are longing to step into the greatness for which God has created them.

Pivot Points

- God calls us beyond the casual, the mundane, and the ordinary to the extraordinary.
- God calls us His sons and daughters. He greatly desires that we walk in the revelation of that knowledge—that truth.
- God calls us into His greatness to know the extravagance of His love and to step into a life of trust and faith in Christ alone.
- God calls us to leave our fears, our defeat, our setbacks, and our failures behind and gaze into the face of Jesus and hear these life-giving words: "So if the Son sets you free, you will be free indeed" (John 8:36, ESV).

Let's pray:

Father, thank You for creating me with wonder, awe, and greatness that comes from Your very nature living in me. You have filled me with dignity, honor, and glory. Father, help me to see myself as You see me. I ask that You would remove every barrier that would keep me from living from that truth. Lord, You say that the truth will set me free; I want to live in the truth that allows me to live as one of Your beloved children. Father, I want to experience Your love, kindness, and greatness, to behold You as my Papa, who believes the best, sees the best, and desires the best for me. Amen!

LET'S TALK ABOUT IT

Chuck Pierce, in his book, ***Time To Defeat The Devil*** stated, "There is a place called 'Beyond' that the Lord is calling us to." What does that mean to you?

What is the key to going beyond? What does it mean to fix our eyes on Jesus? What are some ways we do that?

What does it mean that we are destined for greatness in light of Ephesians 1:19?

According to Psalm 139:13-14, how does God see us? Why is it important to know who we are in Christ that leads to an overcoming, victorious life?

What are you asking God to do in light of the purpose of this book (p 8-9)?

Which of the Pivot Points speaks to you? How and in what way?

What one thing can you take away from this lesson?

Lesson 2

GOING BEYOND WHEN THE CREEK DRIES UP

⌘

We find in 1 Kings 17:1-7 that the Lord leads Elijah beside the Brook Cherith where the ravens take care of him. Ravens usually live in pairs, but can be seen working cooperatively to feed Elijah. While he is hidden away, God is cutting away things from Elijah's heart. The name "Cherith" means *to remove or to cut away*. We all come to those places where God does surgery on the heart, not to wound us, but to heal us. He teaches us how to go beyond when our present circumstances are not the most pleasant and even a bit uncomfortable. These are not places where He keeps us, but places where He hides us so He can do something deep within our hearts that brings glory to His name. God has some things to cut away from Elijah's heart during this period. But, God is also depositing things of His Spirit into Elijah that prepare him for the days ahead. God's call upon Elijah destines him for greatness.

When you find the creek dried up in your life, it is a time when God develops the message and the messenger; it is a time of hiddenness when not much is happening outwardly.

For times like this, Jesus says, "Whatever I tell you in the dark, speak in the light; and what you hear in the ear, preach on the housetops" (Matthew 10:27).

Before revival comes, there may be times of drought—a time when words from God are scarce—when heaven seems silent. During this time, we can become complacent and predictable as the prophet Amos describes: "'Behold, the days are coming,' says the Lord God, 'that I will send a famine on the land, not a famine of bread, nor a thirst for water, but of hearing the words of the Lord'" (Amos 8:11).

When we face our darkest hour—when we have been met with a great challenge in our lives—when it seems all is lost, God is just beginning. Our turnaround is coming. God takes the crisis where we find ourselves lacking, and He begins to turn it around. God takes us beyond those places of hiddenness and those times of quiet retreat where we are feeding on what comes into our lives to a place where He can use us.

This chapter highlights the challenges we face when what we have been trusting in dries up. We are given a Word from the Lord that this season is over, and He is taking us to yet another season in our walk with Christ. When one door closes, there is another one waiting for us to walk through. This is the issue Elijah was facing.

Where God Guides, He Provides

Paul writes, "And my God shall supply all your need according to His riches in glory by Christ Jesus" (Philippians 4:19). God uses the most unusual ways to feed us and provide for us. It is when we learn to be obedient in the small things that God gives to us what will take us beyond so more will come.

God says, "I have commanded the ravens to feed you **there**" (1 Kings 17:4b, emphasis added). The emphasis is on the word "there." The Lord promises that the ravens will feed Elijah as he stays at Cherith. God wants him **there** and will provide for him **there**.

Every bit of food that comes to Elijah comes from the beak of an unclean animal, but God has him **there** only to take him beyond. Just as faithfully as God provides manna for Israel in the wilderness, He provides for Elijah's every need so the prophet can trust in His miraculous provision. Could this be the lesson God is seeking to teach Elijah?

What does this say to us?

Our heavenly Father takes us to those places in our heart to remove—to cut away—the things that impede our obedience and our walk of faith to trust His Word. Things that can impede our growth in Christ are unforgiveness, areas that are not yet surrendered to Him, or areas where we are not walking in victory.

- The Father brings these things to our attention so that He might give us a new, fresh word that **delivers** us, takes us beyond our imagination, and exceeds our expectations.
- Our heavenly Father's message for us and through us is hammered out in the secret place where no one is watching and where He is putting His message in us so that at the right time His message comes forth.

God develops the message and the messenger in the place where we are totally dependent upon Him.

God never intends for us to camp out where the brook has dried up (physically or spiritually) because there is yet more to come. His **desire** is to take us beyond where we cannot presently see to the place where clarity of vision is developed, and He deploys us with His message, mandate, and prophetic Word on our lips.

Elijah obediently goes to the Brook Cherith where he is fed by the ravens, and God develops the message and the messenger as he learns dependence upon Him. The name *Elijah* means "Yahweh is my God," and that is the message God imparts into the heart of Elijah. This same message must become our testimony: "The Lord is our God."

This is not only a place where Elijah experiences the provision of God; it would also be a place where God dries up that provision as He delivers something new. God releases a fresh wind of revelation about the Father's heart—a word that not only sustained him, but would also be a word that sustains others, as well.

Releasing a New Word

Jesus says, "'The words that I speak to you are spirit, and they are life'" (John 6:63b). What God is imparting to Elijah during this time at the brook are words of life to others. The Lord further explains: "'For out of the abundance of the heart the mouth speaks'" (Matthew 12:34b). God is filling Elijah with the capacity to carry what He will do in the lives of others. For example, Elijah confronts the prophets of Baal, moving the people of God to choose whom they will believe, God or Baal. This fresh word brought the people to the point of decision and faith to choose God.

What God declares to Elijah while in the secret place came to the light as he boldly proclaims the Word of God and demonstrates the power of God. There may be times God is unable to release a new word because we are camped out at a place where the brook is dried up. God is basically saying, *"I want to take you beyond to receive a fresh, new revelation of My heart."*

Let us not be content to remain in the place where the brook has dried up, but to lay hold of God's grace that will take us where we cannot go on our own. Through the strength He gives to our inner man, God takes us beyond.

What Does This Mean?

- When the brook dries up, it does not mean the end. There is yet more to come.
- When the brook dries up, it has nothing to do with disobedience. Elijah goes to that brook in obedience to God, and it dries up when that season is over.

The brook represents all the dry places in our lives, but God is there with words of encouragement, direction, plans, and purposes for us. He will take us beyond as we keep our eyes on Jesus.

Elijah was getting ready to step into a new season. When resources dry up and when circumstances seem to shout so loudly, do something. When you are tired and exhausted, and your inner resources are depleted, what do you do, and how do you respond?

> Waiting on God is one of the hardest things in this world to do. That means virtually doing nothing until He gives the signal. Part of the genius of Elijah is that he did nothing until God gave the word. (R. T. Kendal, ***These Are the Days of Elijah*** [2]).

James writes, "And [Elijah] prayed again, and the heavens gave rain, and the earth produced its fruit" (James 5:18). God may close one door only to open another one. When the brook dries up, you have to ask, "What is God saying?".

Bible scholar and teacher, F.B. Meyer addresses the question: "Why does God let the brook dry up?"

> He wants to teach us to trust in Him. He wants to empty us of ourselves, as He emptied the apostles by ten days of waiting before Pentecost. He wants to loosen our roots so He can lead us to other spheres of service, ministry, experiences, expressions and influence. He wants to contrast the brook that dries up to a river that never ceases (***Elijah: And The Secret Of His Power***[3]).

This is what it means for God to take us beyond our last experience and the last word from Him to the next word He has for us that is life-giving and filled with hope and promise. Walking in our destiny of greatness is learning to walk in the present word that God has given to us and to live from that word. It is learning to live in the now.

The Call to Move Forward

There had been no rain in the land because of Elijah's prayer. When God is ready, when the land is ready, when the hearts are ready, and when the messenger is ready, God pours out the rain of His Spirit. When that season of cutting away is over, God immediately leads Elijah to a village called Zarephath where he encounters a widow for whom God supernaturally provides oil and flour that never runs out until the rains return (1 Kings 17:14-16). This same widow's son later dies and is raised from the dead (1 Kings 17:21-24).

This place of miracles becomes the fruit of the secret place where God develops a message and a messenger at Cherith. God is taking Elijah beyond the place that has dried up to a place of abundant supply where supernatural provision is given.

God desires that we move forward, not backward. He doesn't want us to stay where we are, but to go beyond. God gives us new models of ministry, He gives us new expressions of worship, He gives us a fresh word for a new season, and He gives us new leadings of the Holy Spirit. He says to us, *"I will take you beyond where you thought you could never get."* He says, *"I will turn your mourning into dancing (Psalm 30:11), and the places where you experienced defeat, I will take you beyond to victory."*

Pivot Points

- God conceals us for a time as He performs a deeper work in our hearts.
- God dries up what we have been trusting in order to provoke us to further leadings of His Spirit.
- God always has another word for us when we are ready to receive it.
- Where God leads us, He always makes provision for us there to trust Him.
- When we are ready, the circumstances are ready, and when God is ready, He releases the message He has deposited in us by His Spirit to others.

Let's pray:

Father, Help me to discern your seasons and cooperate with them. I choose to make You my Provider as I declare that You are the One who supplies all my need. There is no shortage in Your Kingdom. Father, I ask for Your forgiveness for living with a poverty spirit (thinking small, believing small, and expecting small). Father, I thank You for Your generous Spirit that makes all grace abound toward me. I declare that You make me sufficient for every good work, and I stand in lack of no good thing. Amen.

LET'S TALK ABOUT IT

What does it mean when the creek dries up?

Why is it important to be open to the next word God has for us?

What does the word "beyond" mean to you?

Why is it important to know when God is taking us from one season in our life to another season?

How are we to respond to those times?

When has there been a time in your life when the brook dried up, and what was your response?

Which of the Pivot Points speaks to you? How and in what way?

What one thing can you take away from this lesson?

Lesson 3

BEYOND OUR DROUGHT TO FRUITFULNESS

⌘

At the onset of the drought, Elijah obediently goes to the Brook Cherith where the ravens feed him. It is in that place where he is totally dependent upon God. The drought is not just about judgment on a nation that turned to idolatry, but it also demonstrates that Baal, who is considered "lord of the rain," is powerless to give rain. It shows there is none like the LORD; He is God. When the brook dries up, it may be God's way of getting our attention.

At the closing of one season, God does a new thing that moves us forward. We see in the book of Isaiah that it says: "Do not remember the former things, nor consider the things of old. Behold, I will do a new thing, now it springs forth; shall you not know it? (Isaiah 43:18-19a). God will take seasons of drought and bring new life with the rain of His Spirit. It is prayer that takes us from one season to another.

Going beyond for Elijah is going from the place that becomes dry and empty to a place where floods sweep over the dry ground of his heart. God will pour out His Spirit to all who come hungry and thirsty for Him.

This chapter is about passionate, persevering prayer that demonstrates we will do whatever it takes to get the heart of God. The pouring out of His heart leads to new beginnings. Transitions begin to take place, breakthroughs are within sight, and God begins to take us to the place called "Beyond."

> Then Elijah said to Ahab, "Go up, eat and drink; for there is the sound of abundance of rain." So Ahab went up to eat and drink. And Elijah went up to the top of Carmel; then he bowed down on the ground, and put his face between his knees, and said to his servant, "Go up now, look toward the sea." So he went up and looked, and said, "There is nothing." And seven times he said, "Go again." Then it came to pass the seventh time that he said, "There is a cloud, as small as a man's hand, rising out of the sea!" So he said, "Go up, say to Ahab, 'prepare your chariot, and go down before the rain stops you'"(1 Kings 18:41-44).

God takes Elijah from the brook that dries up to a river that never ceases: "I will pour water on him who is thirsty, and floods on dry ground; I will pour [out] My Spirit" (Isaiah 44:3). The river of God is a place where we touch the heart of God and where the heart of God touches us: "He shall be like a tree planted by the rivers of water, that brings forth its fruit in its season" (Psalm 1:3a). Jesus says, "He who abides in me, and I in him, bears much fruit" (John 15:5).

In the book entitled ***Defining Moments,*** Bill Johnson relates the experience of Roland and Heidi Baker, who have experienced the overflow of God's Spirit:

> Heidi and Roland Baker, missionaries to Mozambique, say few things happened the first seventeen years there. Then she and her husband attended Toronto Airport Christian Fellowship where Randy Clark was preaching a revival. Heidi said, "Randy Clark pointed his finger at me and asked, 'Do you want Mozambique?'" She said at that moment, "The heavenly fire of God began to fall upon me. I was so hot I literally thought I was going to burn up and die." Heidi said, "I was unable to move for seven days. Her husband, Roland, had to carry her to the hotel and back to the meetings each day." She goes on to say, "The weight of His glory was upon me, I was utterly helpless." In seventeen previous years they had planted four churches. Since her encounter with God, they have planted over 6,000 churches in eight years[4].

The river of God opens the heart to the things of God. Luke tells this story: "Now a certain woman named Lydia heard us. She was a seller of purple from the city of Thyatira, who worshiped God. The Lord **opened** her heart to heed the things spoken by Paul" (Acts 16:14, emphasis added). Lydia was now able to understand and do what Paul had spoken. To ***open*** is *to make our hearts completely accessible*. This word "open" is also used in Luke 24:31-32, 45 where Jesus **opens** the hearts and eyes of the disciples to see Him; He **opens** the Scriptures to them and their understanding that they might comprehend it. **Let our lives be planted by the river of God so that fruit may abound.**

Let us experience the renewal of His life-giving Spirit. Let us continually be refreshed by His Spirit. Let us be a people through whom the river of God's Spirit flows in a mighty way.

Let us open our hearts and lives to all that God has for us as He takes us to that place called "Beyond."

Praying With Passion

In this life, it is clear there can be things that weigh us down, there can be walls that keep us from experiencing breakthrough, and there can be mountains we can't get over. However, God desires that we be a people of prayer—mighty in prayer—a people who move those mountains. Jesus tells us to speak to the mountains in our way; He instructs us on how to remove our obstacles through faith and boldness when He says:

> "Whoever says to this mountain, 'Be removed and be cast into the sea,' and does not doubt in his heart, but believes that those things he says will be done, he will have whatever he **says**." (Mark 11:23, emphasis added).

There is one word that is mentioned three times in this verse, and it is the word "says." The meaning is to say something, to speak, to verbalize, to declare, or to command. We must learn to speak our faith and our deliverance in accordance with God's Word. Following Jesus' resurrection, He, "also presented Himself alive…being seen by them during forty days and **speaking** of the things pertaining to the kingdom of God" (Acts 1:3, emphasis added). Jesus speaks words of life to those around Him, and things begin to change.

When Elijah feels the release to pray again, God opens up the heavens as he "bowed down on the ground, and put his face between his knees...Then it came to pass" (1 Kings 18:42b, 44a, emphasis added). Elijah speaks passionately, and he prays passionately.

To pray passionately means to speak, say, declare the deep feelings and thoughts of the heart. When deep feelings of the heart are verbally expressed from our mind through our mouth, this becomes prayer.

Lessons from Hannah

Hannah is one who feels deeply and who expresses the deep desires of her heart. However, she cannot get beyond a sense of rejection, failure, and emptiness. Hannah pours her heart out to God in prayer. The Lord responds to her desperate cry; He is about to take her beyond that.

> As she was praying to the Lord, Eli watched her. Seeing her lips moving but hearing no sound, he thought she had been drinking. "Must you come here drunk?" he demanded. "Throw away your wine!" "Oh no, sir!" she replied. "I haven't been drinking wine or anything stronger. But I am very discouraged, and I was pouring out my heart to the Lord. Don't think I am a wicked woman! For I have been praying out of great anguish and sorrow."
>
> "In that case," Eli said, "go in peace! May the God of Israel grant the request you have asked of him." "Oh, thank you, sir!" she exclaimed. Then she went back and began to eat again, and she was no longer sad (1 Samuel 1:12-18, NLT).

Let's examine Hannah's experience here. The **first** thing we learn about Hannah is that she is at a place in her life where she could no longer be passive concerning her mountain. Scripture says, "Hannah was in deep anguish, crying bitterly as she prayed to the Lord" (1 Samuel 1:10, NLT). Hannah's attitude was, *"I'm not going to let go of God until He answers my prayer."* As Christians, we need to go to the Lord resolute in our prayers and commitments.

The **second** thing we learn about Hannah is that she comes to the place where she pours out her heart before the Lord. Eli, the priest, thinks she has been drinking, but Hannah tells him: "[I have] **poured** out my soul before the Lord...for out of the abundance of my complaint and grief I have spoken until now" (1 Samuel 1:15b-16b, emphasis added). She is praying passionately for a breakthrough to go beyond the critical words of others that have wounded her spirit. The Psalmist encourages us, "**Pour** out your heart before Him; God is a refuge for us" (Psalm 62:8b, emphasis added). It's at this moment that things begin to change for Hannah.

The atmosphere around her becomes filled with the presence of God, and the wind of the Spirit stirs within her. Her change is about to come, and the Lord is taking her to a place called beyond her sorrow, grief, and barrenness to a place of fruitfulness, blessing, and promise.

In that precise moment when Eli speaks words of hope, promise, comfort, and strength, there is an impartation to Hannah. He declares, "Go in peace, and the God of Israel grant your petition which you have asked of Him" (1 Samuel 1:17). The miracle she desires is about to come to pass. Jesus says, "Therefore I say to you, whatever things you ask when you pray, believe that you receive them, and you will have them" (Mark 11:24).

The **third** thing we learn about Hannah is that she comes to the place where she walks in the peace of God: "So the woman went her way and ate, and her face was no longer sad. Then they rose in the morning and worshiped before the Lord" (1 Samuel 1:18b-19a).

The Bible states, "So it came to pass in the process of time that Hannah conceived and bore a son, called his name Samuel, saying, 'because I have asked for him from the Lord'" (1 Samuel 1:20). Samuel means "heard by God." The mountain for Hannah is her barrenness and the ridicule she receives because of it. God lifts the mountain of ridicule, shame, and failure from her and comes to her aid. He hears her passionate prayer and allows her to witness God's grace for a new beginning because He is taking her to the place called "Beyond."

Watch the progression as Hannah encountered the Lord's grace and goodness:

- Hannah receives God's word from Eli by faith.
  "So the woman went her way and ate" (1 Samuel 1:18).
- Hannah's response to God's word brings a great joy that speaks of hope and promise.
  "And her face was no longer sad" (v. 18).
- Hannah **rests** in God's word that He will bring it forth at the right time which results in gratitude and thanksgiving.
  "Then they rose early in the morning and worshiped before the Lord..." (v. 19).

Passionate prayer originates in the heart, is conveyed to the mind, and is spoken through our voice.

Passionate prayer changes events, history, and circumstances, and it mobilizes all of heaven to move mountains. There is a place the Lord is leading you to called "Beyond." See it and start pressing toward that place! Going beyond is a place of lifting—where God lifts the burdens, failures, setbacks, and disappointments; He lightens our load so that we can go to the place called "Beyond."

Pivot Points

- God looks for places to pour out His Spirit upon dry, parched, and hungry hearts.
- God calls us beyond our disappointments, frustrations, and feelings of defeat to a place where we enter His rest, and where we trust Him for the outcome.
- God is looking for those who will pray until something happens. They see it in God's Word, and then pray it into reality.
- God takes our brokenness and sense of defeat and brings us to a place of worship, sacrifice, and great joy.

God calls us to speak to the mountains in our lives so that we can learn to live an overcoming and victorious life through the power of the Holy Spirit.

Let's pray:

Father, thank You for bringing me to those places in life where I trust You completely for the outcome. Those places where You give me the courage to stand on the promises of Your Word and watch You bring them to pass. Father, help me to pray boldly, courageously, and passionately until my change comes, and Your Kingdom is advanced. Amen.

LET'S TALK ABOUT IT

What does it mean to be planted like a tree by the river (Psalm 1:3)? What does the river represent?

How does Elijah's passionate prayer begin to change the drought to a river?

What does it mean to speak to the mountains in our lives? To what mountains do you need to start speaking?

What does it mean for Hannah to go "beyond?"

How happens when we pour out our hearts before the Lord? How does that begin to change our situation?

Which of the Pivot Points speaks to you? How and in what way?

What is one thing you can take away from this lesson?

Lesson 4

GOING BEYOND WHERE WE CANNOT SEE

⌘

Abraham is referred to as the father of our faith (Romans 4:16) because he believed, and it was counted to him as righteousness (Genesis 15:6). Abraham is called to go beyond the worship of idols to placing his faith in El Shaddai, God Almighty, who is mightier than all his foes (Genesis 17:1). Abraham and Sarah are called to go beyond their barrenness in old age and bring forth the promise of God to make Abraham's seed as stars in the sky (Genesis 15:5). Abraham is called to go beyond **his** ability to see **God's** ability by obeying the Word of God as he offers up his only son, Isaac, as a sacrifice. In doing this, he discovers that God will be his provider. The Bible records, "And Abraham called the name of the place, The-Lord-Will-Provide" (Genesis 22:14). Abraham presses into God as he hears His call to go beyond where he is to a land that God will show him which He promises to give to him and his descendants for a possession (Acts 7:3, 5). Abraham's faith is tested in three areas that call him to go beyond where he could see to the place that God will take him, a place called "Beyond."

This chapter is about trusting God's leadership when He gives us enough information to take only one step at a time. It is about believing that God is

Almighty, and nothing is impossible with Him. It is about leaving what we know and taking hold of what God has for us.

---

1) The Test of Leaving

The first calling of Abraham is in Mesopotamia, in Ur of Chaldea. Stephen says, "The God of glory appeared to our father Abraham while he was in Mesopotamia before he dwelt in Haran" (Acts 7:2). From this we see that God calls Abraham before he left Ur. The very God of glory appears to Abraham and calls him out of his country, his kindred, and his father's house into the land that God will show him. In Genesis 12, God calls Abraham a second time:

> Now the Lord had said to Abram: "Get out of your country, from your family and from your father's house, to a land that I will show you. I will make you a great nation; I will bless you and make your name great; and you shall be a blessing. I will bless those who bless you, and I will curse him who curses you; and in you all the families of the earth shall be blessed." So Abram departed as the Lord had spoken to him, and Lot went with him. And Abram was seventy-five years old when he departed from Haran (Genesis 12:1-4).

This calling is the same as the original calling. He hears the first call in Ur which only brings him halfway. The second call in Haran brings him all the way into Canaan.

Haran is the place where Abram stops short. In Hebrew, "Haran" means "crossroads" and describes a place of decision.

God also brings us to a place called Haran—a crossroads—a place of decision—to follow God or not. Abraham is faced with such a decision. Will he stay there, stopping short of God's call and destiny upon his life, or will he trust God to proceed? If Abraham refuses to go any further, the rest of the Old Testament would not have existed.

The way to move into your future is leaving your past behind. Jesus says, "No one, having put his hand to the plow, and looking back, is fit for the kingdom of God" (Luke 9:62). Abraham's encounter with God catapults him into his destiny and God's purpose. God does not want us to stop short of His call upon our lives.

Bill Johnson, in his book ***Face to Face with God***, observes, "Abraham left the human boundaries that defined his life and stepped into a journey of total dependence on God's perspective and commands."[5]

Faith is choosing boldly and unswervingly to believe what God has said. We release the creative power of God's Word by believing it even in the face of challenging circumstances. God takes us beyond our doubts, fears, and anxieties as we press toward the place called "Beyond."

In Acts 7:1-7, we see that God calls Abraham while he is still living in Mesopotamia before he dwells in Haran. Abraham pitches a tent between Bethel and Ai, and he builds an altar there. Let's look at the significance of this.

Abraham is building spiritual experiences into his life—places where God impacts His life. *Bethel* comes from the

Hebrew word meaning "House of God." *Ai* means "heap of ruins." This is a prophetic statement by Abraham concerning his life. The choice illustrated here is to choose the way of the Lord—the way of blessing and fruitfulness—or to choose to go our own way and come to our own ruin and barrenness. Like Abraham, we stand at places of decision regarding choices, places, and crossroads. We want to be wise, like Abraham, and choose the way of God.

God will take us beyond the place of barrenness to the place of fruitfulness and blessing, but we must choose to let Him take us to that place. As a wealthy man, Abraham risks all to follow God. This godly leader is willing to risk everything on God's faithfulness and venture into the unknown to receive the Promised Land that God will give to him and his descendants. Abraham chooses to walk through to the victory, and he builds altars along the way to memorialize God's leading. By doing this, he chooses to step into the "Beyond."

2) The Test of Trusting

This is God's promise to Abraham: "I will make you exceedingly fruitful; and I will make nations of you, and kings shall come from you" (Genesis 17:6). The Bible states, "When Abram was ninety-nine years old, the Lord appeared to Abram and said to him, 'I am Almighty God; walk before Me and be blameless...and will multiply you exceedingly" (Genesis 17:1-2). God wants Abraham to know Him as El Shaddai, Almighty God, who is able to do far above what he could ever think or believe could happen on his own.

What does it mean to know God as Almighty? It is that place of humility where we can experience the greatness of God and His unlimited resources. It is that place where God changes our name and our nature. It is that place where God speaks promise and destiny into our lives. God is mighty and will save us from getting stuck and will enable us to go beyond whatever difficulty, challenge, or adversity we may face. **God is our mighty Father.**

Let this be our confession:

- He is mighty to save to the uttermost (Isaiah 63:1b, NLT).
- He is mighty to strengthen us by His Spirit in our inner man (Ephesians 3:16).
- He is mighty in battle for the battle is not ours, but His. We can stand and see the salvation of the Lord (Psalm 24:8).
- He is mighty to deliver us from everything that keeps us from advancing in the Kingdom of God (Amos 2:14).
- He is mighty in our midst; He will never leave us nor forsake us (Zephaniah 3:17).
- He is mighty in us because greater is He who is in you than the enemy who is in the world (2 Corinthians 13:3; 1 John 4:4).

Continuing on in Abraham's story. Let's look from the time this promise is given to Sarah to the fulfillment of it. **First** of all, Sarah's barrenness is broken with a visitation from the Lord. The Bible records:

> And the Lord visited Sarah as He had said, and the Lord did for Sarah as He had spoken. For Sarah conceived and bore Abraham a son in his old age, at the set time of which God had spoken to him (Genesis 21:1-2).

Our change comes with a visitation of God's presence upon our brokenness, our barrenness, our emptiness, and our failures.

A visitation of God:

- Will come to those who have **prepared** for His visitation through prayer and openness to what God is presently doing. It comes when we recognize our need for His presence.
- Will come to those who will **receive** God moving even if it doesn't make sense, and we don't understand it. It comes when we least expect it, but we welcome it.
- Will come to those who will **step out** and take risks. It comes when unbelief gives place to faith to believe God when surrounded by challenges.

Second, Sarah's barrenness comes to an end when she trusts the Word of the Lord. God tells her, "Is anything too hard for the Lord? At the appointed time I will return to you, according to the time of life, and Sarah shall have a son" (Genesis 18:14).

Frank Damazio writes in ***From Barrenness to Fruitfulness***, "The more difficult the fulfillment (of the promise), the more powerful and wonderful will be our matured faith.

Faith grows by going through the tests, the seasons of delay and the silence."[6] The Bible affirms this thought that it is "through faith and patience [we} inherit the promises" (Hebrews 6:12b).

By believing the promise of God, He becomes responsible to bring it forth. He's greater than all of our doubts, and He's always on time. Our attitude of faith is to remain steadfast.

Third, Sarah's barrenness is broken when she waits on God's timing: "For Sarah conceived and bore Abraham a son in his old age, at the **set time** of which God had spoken to him" (Genesis 21:2, emphasis added). This is a reference back to Genesis 17:21 which says, "But My covenant I will establish with Isaac, whom Sarah shall bear to you at this **set time** next year" (emphasis added).

What can we take away from tests that come our way?

We trust God's Word to bring forth His promises in His time, and we believe that divine delays work for our good and His glory. We stand believing and confessing: "Nothing is too difficult for God" (Jeremiah 32:17, AMP).

3) The Test of Surrendering

> Then He said "Take now your son, your only son Isaac, whom you love, and go to the land of Moriah, and offer him there as a burnt offering on one of the mountains of which I shall tell you."...And Abraham called the name of the place, The-Lord-Will-Provide; as it is said to this day, "In the Mount of the Lord it shall be provided" (Genesis 22:2, 14).

Abraham's test is going beyond where he cannot see to the knowledge that God would be His provider. Going beyond allows God to show us His nature and reveal His character. It is where we learn that God is absolutely faithful and trustworthy; all that He has for us is good.

What Are You Facing?

Are you facing the need to be bold and exercise faith when it would be easier to play it safe and be cautious? Is it the need to trust God to make a way where there seems to be no way at this time? Is it the need to surrender when it would be easier to clutch on to what is yours? **Why is this test of surrender so powerful?**

Abraham is surrendering his future to the Lord. He is leaning into all the promises God gave to him. He is surrendering everything in a way that goes against logic and good sense. He is surrendering those things that are most precious and rewarding to him. For Abraham comes to God believing that He is, and that "He is a rewarder of those who diligently seek Him" (Hebrews 11:6b).

Throughout our lives, faith develops as we are confronted with tests. Our tests vary in seasons and duration but, rest assured, God is at work. We find in the Bible this verse: "Until the time that [Joseph's] word came to pass, the word of the Lord tested him" (Psalm 105:19). The word "tested" refers to the years of character development before the fulfillment of God's promises. Our faith grows, and our character is honed as we pass the tests of leaving, trusting, and surrendering to God's will and plan.

From the time Abraham is called out of Mesopotamia to the time Isaac is born is 25 years. We can wait 15 minutes, or maybe a day for a change to happen. A week or a month is really stretching us, but 25 years to see a prophetic promise come to fruition is a bit too much for us to handle. But Abraham walks by faith in God who gives him the promise. That's what we should strive to do when our promise is delayed.

The word *delay* means "to cause to be late or slower than expected, or desired, to go or move slowly so that progress is hindered, to put off until a later time" (www.Dictionary.com).

So what is our response to delays? Do we create our own answer, lower the bar and our expectations? Do we simply give up and say, "*It must not have been God's will.*" No, our response to delays must be like Abraham's: we continue to walk in faith toward the promise until it is fulfilled. We go beyond where we cannot see.

Pivot Points

- We must be open to God's leadership in our lives and the new things He wants to do in us and through us.
- We are blessed to be a blessing. We are blessed to be a people that walk by faith and expect God to do what we cannot do on our own.
- Going from the familiar to the unknown can be uncomfortable, but we must know that God's purpose, destiny, and calling upon our lives are greater than our fears and anxieties.

- God's call upon our lives is to trust Him. We trust Him for our salvation; we must also trust Him to lead us through life and to experience His grace, goodness, and provision.
- God desires that we live surrendered lives—surrendered to His highest will and purpose for our lives. Surrender is saying "yes" to God's divine call.

Let's pray:

Father, help me to see beyond where I cannot see. I have not always believed Your promises. I have not always obeyed Your Word, and I have not always waited on Your timing. I ask Your forgiveness for this now. Father, let me experience Your presence and cause faith to arise within me especially when my vision is blurred. Father, give me confident hope to wait for You to unfold Your promise and demonstrate your power because I believe nothing is too hard for You. Amen!

LET'S TALK ABOUT IT

Why do we have to leave some things behind in order to step into our destiny?

What does it mean for Abraham to go beyond when his faith is being tested?

What makes surrender so powerful? What does surrender mean to you?

What did trust mean to Abraham?

What does trust mean to you? For what are you presently trusting God?

Which of the Pivot Points speaks to you? How and in what way?

What one thing can you take away from this lesson?

Lesson 5

BEYOND PROMISE GIVEN TO PROMISE FULFILLED

⌘

Twenty-five years pass from the time Abraham is called out of Mesopotamia to the time Isaac is born. We can wait 15 minutes or maybe a day. A week or a month is really stretching us, but 25 years for a change to happen and to see prophetic promises coming to fruition would be a bit too much to handle. The word delay means, "To cause to be late or slower than expected or desired, to go or move slowly so that progress is hindered, to put off until a later time." So what is our response to delays? Create our own answer, lower the bar and our expectations, or to simply give up and say, "It must not have been God's will?"

This chapter is about the timing of God and seeing those long-awaited promises come to pass. It is about receiving times of God's visitation that bring hope, promise, and new beginnings. It is about moving from barrenness to fruitfulness for nothing is impossible with God.

> Then they (angels) said to him, "Where is Sarah your wife?" So he said, "Here, in the tent." And He said, "I will certainly return to you according to the time of life, and behold, Sarah your wife shall have a son." (Sarah was listening in the tent door which was

behind him.) Now Abraham and Sarah were old, well advanced in age; and Sarah had passed the age of childbearing.

Therefore Sarah laughed within herself, saying, "After I have grown old, shall I have pleasure, my lord being old also?" And the Lord said to Abraham, "Why did Sarah laugh, saying, 'Shall I surely bear a child, since I am old?' Is anything too hard for the Lord? At the appointed time I will return to you, according to the time of life, and Sarah shall have a son." But Sarah denied it, saying, "I did not laugh," for she was afraid. And He said, "No, but you did laugh! (Genesis 18:9-15).

The Promise Given, The Promise Fulfilled

First of all, the promise is fulfilled when Sarah's barrenness comes to an end with a visitation from the Lord: "And the Lord visited Sarah as He had said, and the Lord did for Sarah as He had spoken. For Sarah conceived and bore Abraham a son in his old age, at the set time of which God had spoken to him" (Genesis 21:1-2).

Our change comes with a visitation of God's presence upon our brokenness, our barrenness, our emptiness, and our human failures.

A **visitation of God** will come to those who have **prepared** for it through prayer and openness to what God is presently doing. When we recognize our need for God's presence, He will come to those who will **receive** Him He comes even if it doesn't make sense to us at the time, and we don't understand it, or when we least expect it, but we welcome Him. It will come to those who will step out and take risks.

When risk gives place to faith, we wholeheartedly believe God even when surrounded by challenges. Our prayer is "God visit us, make yourself known to us, let us encounter Your presence and let us see Your glory—Your manifest presence. Let us be refreshed, renewed, and awakened by Your presence. Visit us in such a way that our passion for you makes a habitation for your presence that remains upon us, and we carry Your presence wherever we go."

Let the aroma of Your presence be felt, and experienced by those around us, and we will "glorify God in the day of visitation" (1 Peter 2:12b).

Second, Sarah's barrenness came to an end when she trusted the Word of the Lord. God's response to Sarah is recorded, "Is anything too hard for the Lord? At the **appointed time** I will return to you, according to the time of life, and Sarah shall have a son" (Genesis 18:14, emphasis added). We must lay hold of the appointed time. God has a timetable—an appointed time—for breakthrough. Let us be looking and anticipating for that time. Yet there are times when God is looking for us to make the first move toward Him. It indicates our desire to draw near and to declare the promises of the Lord coming to pass before we see them. Declare God's appointed time for you will come to fruition; it will come to pass. Though it may tarry, God's appointed time will come to pass (Habakkuk 2:3).

> The life of faith is built around promises given, test encountered and fulfillment enjoyed. For every promise, there is a test, and with every test there is grace, mercy and the strength of the Almighty to see us through.
>
> —Frank Damazio
>
> ***From Barrenness to Fruitfulness***[7]

The Bible teaches us, "Through faith and patience [we] inherit the promises" (Hebrews 6:12b). Our attitude and our faith are to be steadfast. Though Abraham and Sarah wait impatiently at times, God honors their faith and gives them the breakthrough they long to see. Sarah's barrenness is broken when she waits on God's timing: "For Sarah conceived and bore Abraham a son in his old age, at the **set time** of which God had spoken to him" (Genesis 21:2, emphasis added). This is a response to the promise given Abraham in Genesis 17:21, "But My covenant I will establish with Isaac, whom Sarah shall bear to you at this set time next year."

Breakthrough Prayer

Our faith life matures when we cooperate through prayer with the promises of God's Word and the joy of those promises coming to pass. We trust God's Word to bring forth His promises in His time and believe that divine delays work for our good and His glory. Our belief and confession are that nothing is too difficult for God.

Breakthrough prayer means steadfastly looking to Jesus, the supplier for our every need. In the midst of our weakness, we find Christ's strength. Paul says, "For when I am weak, then I am strong" (2 Corinthians 12:10b). When we look to Jesus, even in our lack—our unknowing, our weakness—He will provide for us what we don't have in a way that honors Him and brings glory to His name. Breakthrough prayer is an acknowledgment of receiving something from God that only He can give. Abraham is convinced: "My son, God will provide for Himself the lamb for a burnt offering" (Genesis 22:8).

Abraham needs a Word from the Lord that day, not the previous Word, but a new Word for what God is about to do. God speaks twice to Abraham to leave one place and go to another—a place of promise called "Beyond." God calls for him to sacrifice his son; the second time He tells Abraham of His provision. At this point, Abraham holds nothing back. It is not that we don't believe God is our provider. Rather, it is our inability to trust Him to meet us at our point of need. Trust in prayer means that we leave the matter in His hands and take our hands off.

We let Him do something that we can't—something amazing—something life transforming. Total surrender, and placing all our trust in God takes us "Beyond."

Prayer realizes that apart from Him we can do nothing. Give us this day what we need in order to live an overcoming life. It is an acknowledgment of our need for Christ and Christ alone.

We receive the daily supply where God meets us at our point of need, and it becomes a testimony of God's faithfulness. It gives us a testimony of His goodness, grace, and extravagant love. Abraham acknowledges this as he "call[s] the name of the place, The-Lord-Will-Provide *(Jehovah Jireh)*; as it said to this day, 'In the Mount of the Lord it shall be provided" (Genesis 22:14).

Overcoming Faith Requires Three Major Ingredients

> Therefore it is of faith that it might be according to grace, so that the promise might be sure to all the seed, not only to those who are of the law, but also to those who are of the faith of Abraham, who is the father of us all (as it is written, "I have made you a father of many nations") in the presence of Him whom he believed—God, who gives life to the dead and calls those things which do not exist as though they did; who, contrary to hope, in hope believed, so that he became the father of many nations, according to what was spoken, "So shall your descendants be." And not being weak in faith, he did not consider his own body, already dead (since he was about a hundred years old), and the deadness of Sarah's womb. He did not waver at the promise of God through unbelief, but was **strengthened in faith,** giving glory to God, and being fully convinced that what He had promised He was also able to perform. And therefore "it was accounted to him for righteousness" (Romans 4:16-22).

First of all, an overcoming faith submits to the mighty hand of God.

God uses our weakness to show forth His strength. Abraham does not allow his faith in God to vacillate. We see in the above Scripture text: "And not being weak in faith, he did not consider his own body, already dead (since he was about a hundred years old), and the deadness of Sarah's womb" (Romans 4:19). The word translated here as "weak" conveys *the idea of being weak-minded, hesitant, vacillating, doubting, or faint-hearted.* Abraham does the opposite of this; he does not become weak but goes beyond all his doubts, fears, and questions to the place where he humbles himself by pressing into God. Through this, God exalts Abraham to be the father of our faith. Abraham does as Peter exhorts in his Epistle, "Therefore humble yourselves under the mighty hand of God that He may exalt you in due time" (1 Peter 5:6).

Submitting ourselves to the mighty hand of God indicates:

- An issue of the heart.
- Our dependence upon the Lord.
- God's opportunity to intervene on our behalf.

Second, an overcoming faith grows stronger.

"...But was strengthened in faith, giving glory to God, and being fully convinced that what He had promised He was also able to perform" (Romans 4:20b-21).

Abraham grows strong in his faith and is strengthened in faith. Through nearly ten years of waiting for the fulfillment of a seemingly impossible promise, Abraham continues to give glory to God. His faith grows stronger rather than weaker. Abraham gives God the glory for the mighty work He is doing in his life that allows him to see the fruition of God's promise. Abraham is "fully convinced" that God will fulfill His promise. "Fully convinced" means *to fully believe, or to be fully persuaded, to be completely convinced.* God wants us to follow after Abraham.

Being fully convinced means watching the goodness of God unfold before our very eyes.

We know that God has done an eternal work in our lives that no one can take from us. It becomes a testimony from which we live as we declare that God's grace, goodness, and greatness abound upon us, in us, and through us. God gives us a sustaining word to stay the course until everything comes to its appointed time when He will unveil His majesty and glory, and we behold the King of Kings and Lord of Lords.

The Bible teaches the principle of sowing and reaping: "The kingdom of God is as if a man should scatter seed on the ground, and should sleep by night and rise by day, and the seed should sprout and grow he himself does not know how. For the earth yields crops by itself..." (Mark 4:26-28a). What is the importance of sowing seeds according to these verses? We must do our part, and God will do His; we sow and God will give the increase (1 Corinthians 3:7). We don't always understand how He will work, but we know that He will, and it will be good because God is good.

After sowing the seeds God has given, we pray over them as we await our harvest to come. Speak the life of God into those seeds. Declare the hand of God to be upon them. As we live in God's favor, expect increase from what God is already doing. The key to unleashing the promise of God and living in the harvest is to wait patiently for Him. While we look for the harvest, we are reminded to: "rest in the

Lord, and wait patiently for Him" (Psalms 37:7a). As you wait, this is also a time to stir yourselves up in the Lord, to strengthen yourself by beholding Him, and to look to Jesus and away from every distraction until God becomes your focus.

Sometimes, God steps out of His natural laws and works supernaturally on our behalf. In 2 Kings 19, we see God advising Hezekiah how to reap off the uncultivated land to feed His people: "You shall eat this year such as grows of itself [without cultivation], and in the second year what springs from the same; also in the third year sow and reap, plant vineyards and eat the fruit of them...The zeal of the Lord of host will do this" (2 Kings 19:29, 31b). The principle of the earth is sowing and reaping; however, when you mix God's favor with it, there are times when you reap where you do not sow (John 4:38).

A believer who has an overcoming faith is one who submits to the mighty hand of God, who rests, and who increases in faith. It is a believer who knows that God is faithful and watches over His Word to see that it is fulfilled in His way and His time. It is here that we simply say: "Yes, Lord!"

Pivot Points

- Barrenness always brings a crisis into our lives, and God takes it as an opportunity to do something powerful and miraculous.
- The delays of God allow Him time to work on our behalf which enables us to see the larger picture of what He is doing.

- Waiting is God's method of building character and trust in our lives.
- Responding to God's visitation is to welcome Him and to host His presence so that we become a place of habitation.
- Breakthrough prayer is for those of us who are desperate for God to do something new, to act on our behalf, and to propel us into His plan, purpose, and calling.

Let's pray:

Father, I ask that You touch and heal those areas in my life that are barren to bring forth the fruitfulness of Your Spirit. Father, strengthen my faith to believe where I cannot see, and give me a faith that increases in the midst of testing, trials, and waiting. Amen!

LET'S TALK ABOUT IT

What does it mean to come under the mighty hand of God?

Why can we be at peace in the midst of adversity?

According to Romans 4:19-20, what enabled Abraham to go beyond his weakness to strength?

What does breakthrough prayer mean to you? Where do you need a breakthrough?

How can we prepare for a visitation of God in our midst?

Which of the Pivot Points speaks to you? How and in what way?

What one thing can you take away from this lesson?

Lesson 6

BEYOND DISAPPOINTMENT TO DESTINY

⌘

In my youth, I played summer league basketball in hopes of being picked to play on the high school team. I thought if I hustled and showed determination in the midst of taller and bigger guys, they would see my heart to play and that the long, hot hours in the gym would pay off. I remember going over to the wall where the names were posted, and mine was not there. I turned and walked back to the locker disappointed, frustrated, and angry. The question that I kept asking was how could I get beyond this and not remain stuck in my disappointment and frustration?

Moses is in the same boat; he is stuck and cannot get beyond his past heroics. Seeking to be a deliverer, he instead takes the life of another person, and even his own people will not receive him as their leader. Rejected, he finds himself on the backside of the desert as a shepherd for forty years.

This chapter is about how God takes us from those places of disappointment, setback, and disillusionment to stepping into our destiny through a personal encounter with the Lord that changes how we look at ourselves, God, and our future.

> And the Angel of the Lord appeared to him in a flame of fire from the midst of a bush. So he looked, and behold, the bush was burning with fire, but the bush was not consumed. Then Moses said, "I will now turn aside and see this great sight, why the bush does not burn." So when the Lord saw that he turned aside to look, God called to him from the midst of the bush and said, "Moses, Moses!" And he said, "Here I am." Then He said, "Do not draw near this place. Take your sandals off your feet, for the place where you stand is holy ground." Moreover He said, "I am the God of your father—the God of Abraham, the God of Isaac, and the God of Jacob." And Moses hid his face, for he was afraid to look upon God. And the Lord said: "I have surely seen the oppression of My people who are in Egypt, and have heard their cry because of their taskmasters, for I know their sorrows. So I have come down to deliver them out of the hand of the Egyptians, and to bring them up from that land to a good and large land, to a land flowing with milk and honey, to the place of the Canaanites and the Hittites and the Amorites and the Perizzites and the Hivites and the Jebusites (Exodus 3:2-8).

God takes Moses beyond his disappointment to his destiny.

The **first** step of going beyond for Moses is to change his vision. "So he looked, and behold, the bush was burning with fire, but the bush was not consumed" (Exodus 3:2b). Moses took his eyes off himself, his disappointment, his frustration, and his sense of defeat, and lifted his eyes beyond himself to the bush. In going beyond, one of the first things that God does is touch our vision because without vision, we are not able to see God's purpose, direction, and plan for our lives. God wants Moses to shift from looking at himself to looking at Him who was able to take him beyond his disappointments.

God wants Moses to see differently.

God wants us to see how much He **loves** us: "Yes, I have loved you with an everlasting love; therefore with lovingkindness I have drawn you" (Jeremiah 31:3b). One of the first truths we must get into our spirit is how much God loves us. We do not need to prove we are worthy to be loved; we need to realize we stand totally accepted before Abba, Father. Moses needs to know and experience the love of God in order to step into God's purpose, plan, and call upon his life. When there is a love deficiency in our lives, we will do whatever it takes for that emptiness to be filled, even if we look in all the wrong places.

The love of God allows us to lay down the thing that binds us in order to pick up the one thing we need—to know God loves us without measure.

God wants us to see that "He has **removed** our sins as far from us as the east is from the west" (Psalm 103:12, NLT, emphasis mine). When we have a great sense of our sin, we have difficulty receiving forgiveness. Moses may have felt he deserved punishment, so his own self-inflicted punishment was to remove himself far from everyone and everything he had ever known. Many times when we have a sense of our sin, we don't feel capable of being forgiven.

So we continue in the condition or place we are in because turning means change, and change means we cannot wallow in our messes. We must allow God to impart His grace to for us to see as He sees us and for Him to do far beyond what we could ever believe. It is the grace of God that takes us beyond our entrapment and deception to experience God's freedom and the restoring that only He can bring.

God wants us to see His **faithfulness**: "Great is his faithfulness; his mercies begin afresh each morning" (Lamentations 3:23, NLT). In moving beyond, we must know God's faithfulness to not only know His nearness but to realize He is working all things together for our good and His glory. Faithfulness is the very nature and character of God. It goes beyond merely stating He is faithful, for His very person—His makeup—is to be faithful.

We know that because of the Father's faithfulness, He who begins His work in us will complete it (Philippians 1:6). He does not leave us half-healed, but in Him we discover wholeness. He takes our brokenness where we feel we cannot go beyond. God comes and speaks to us in our failings and mistakes to make us see that He is not finished with us. We are His masterpiece, and He is fashioning us after the image of His Son, Jesus.

This is why God touches Moses' viewpoint so that he can lift up his eyes beyond the defeat, the sense of inadequacy, and the rejection he experiences from his own people. The people are offended by his actions and say, "Who made you a ruler and a judge over us?" (Acts 7:27b). Before Moses can go beyond getting ahead of God—beyond trying to make things happen—beyond his last act of presumption—beyond his last disappointment, frustration, rejection, and shame, God must show him that the final word over his life has not yet been spoken; He must give him new vision.

God's purpose for his life was about to change forever, and it came from a bush that was on fire, but not consumed. We all, to some degree or another, have things we cannot get beyond. We get stuck with what was, what could have been, and what should have been, but God says, "*Let me take you beyond what you cannot do in your own strength. Let Me strengthen you.*" We are to live life "forgetting those things which are behind and reaching forward to those things which are ahead" (Philippians 3:13b).

How Does Moses Go Beyond

Moses tells God he can't speak, but the truth is Moses knows very well how to speak for he was "mighty in words and deeds" (Acts 7:22b). So why did Moses say, "I am not eloquent, neither before nor since You have spoken to Your servant; but I am slow of speech and slow of tongue." (Exodus 4:10)?

The answer is the things that happen to us can rob us of our voice (our confidence, our sense of worth, our value), and we feel we have nothing to contribute. Failure, shame, and disappointment can rob us of what God has put in our hearts to do. Moses makes up excuses why God needs to choose someone else to deliver His people from the harsh treatment of Pharaoh because he possibly feels like a failure.

Moses cannot get beyond what he is feeling and what he experiences; He needs an encounter with God.

We **first** need to take another step and leave behind our last step so we can go beyond. The thing that holds us back from the next step, from going beyond, may possibly be our previous step—we can't get beyond our last step which may have been painful. It may have been a loss, or it could have been as simple as our hopes met with disappointment, but it stopped us. Moses needs to go beyond—to take another step—to encounter Abba Father. Like Moses, we need to step into God's purpose and plan to see our hopes and our dreams come to pass. We must offer to the Lord the things that brought us to where we are so that He can take us to where He wants us to be.

This is where many of us live—stuck and unable to go beyond our disappointments, our failures, our frustrations, and all of our good intentions being misunderstood. We struggle to get beyond these things. The only way to go beyond these things is through a personal encounter with the Lord and what He says about our lives, our purpose, and our calling. We must allow Him to give us a renewed vision of what He is doing now. The first step of going beyond for Moses is that God needs to touch his vision: "Moses saw it, he marveled at the sight" (Acts 7:31a).

The **second** step in going beyond is to draw near to God as Luke records: "And as he **drew near** to observe, the voice of the Lord came to him" (Acts 7:31b, emphasis added). More details are included in the Exodus account:

> So when the Lord saw that he turned aside to look, God called to him from the midst of the bush and said, "Moses, Moses!" And he said, "Here I am." Then He said, "Do not **draw near** this place. Take your sandals off your feet, for the place where you are standing is holy ground" (Exodus 3:4b-5, emphasis added).

This sight of a bush burning stirs an intense desire in Moses to draw near. This is the "divine tug" of God upon the heart to draw closer.

God demands that Moses **humble** himself in the presence of His holiness. James writes, "Humble yourselves in the sight of the Lord, and He will lift you up" (James 4:10). Moses will not redeem the people of God by his own hand as he thinks (Acts 7:25), but God Himself **redeems** His people and brings them out of slavery into the Promised Land by working through Moses.

We lay aside our steps, our ways, and our thoughts so that we might walk in His steps, His ways, and have His thoughts about what He is doing. God tells Moses, "Take your sandals off your feet, for the place where you stand is holy ground" (Acts 7:33). God always gives us a place to stand in His presence. Moses is required to remove His sandals in order to be in step with the Lord. He has to see what God is doing in his life and accept His calling. Isaiah describes well what Moses was experiencing: "Behold, I will do a new thing, now it shall spring forth; shall you not know it? I will even make a road in the wilderness and rivers in the desert" (Isaiah 43:19).

God was saying, "I am getting ready to do something new, and I am inviting you to co-labor with Me. After what has been a wilderness experience for you over the last forty years, I am releasing My Spirit which brings a refreshing, a renewing, and a restoring of all things."

It's only in His presence that we **discover** God has something to say to us and that He knows our names. God knows Moses name: "Moses, Moses…I am the God of your father" (Exodus 3:4, 6). This is what "personal encounter" means. God knows our names, and He has something of value to say to us and impart in us. This is the beginning of going beyond. **Remember our destiny is not our destination; our destiny is in what we are becoming as we give our lives to the Lord.**

We **take hold** of the promise of God that says, "Draw near to God and He will draw near to you" (James 4:8). We do this in three ways:

- draw near in child-like faith (Mark 10:14-15).
- draw near with confidence (Hebrews 4:16).
- draw near for it is the place of blessing, provision, and seeing the works of God.

Drawing closer to God is a significant part of our personal encounter with Him. The psalmist writes, "But it is good to draw near to God; I have put my trust in the Lord God, that I may declare all Your works (Psalm 73:28).

The name *Moses* means to "draw out." He is drawn out of the waters of the Nile so that he can draw near to the presence of God at the burning bush.

We go beyond where we are to the place where God wants us to be so that He might speak to us, encourage us, and transform us.

The key to going beyond is this verse: "Now to Him who is able to do exceedingly abundantly above all that we ask or think, according to the power that works in us" (Ephesians 3:20). The phrase "exceedingly abundantly above" means *beyond*. God is able to take us beyond all that we ask, think, or even believe according to His power that works within us.

Moses steps from rejection to being chosen .

> This Moses, whom they rejected saying, "Who made you a ruler and a judge?" Is the one God sent to be a ruler and a deliverer by the hand of the Angel who appeared to him in the bush. He brought them out, after he had shown wonders and signs in the land of Egypt, and in the Red Sea, and in the wilderness forty years (Acts 7:35-36).

God wants Moses to walk into his destiny and his "beyond," but he first needs an encounter with the One who loves him the most. He cannot go beyond because he interprets the events in his life as punishment. He sees God as the judge and jury who gives him a forty-year sentence to the backside of the desert.

This scene can remind us of Adam and Eve after they are deceived by the serpent (the devil). When they hear the sound of the Lord walking in the garden, they hide themselves from the presence of the Lord God among the trees of the garden because they are afraid (Genesis 3:8b, 10). **Fear keeps us from going beyond.**

God wants Moses to see Him because He is going to give him a new picture—a new frame of reference. God wants Moses to know that He is for him not against him. Like Moses, we may see the times when we do wrong, when we miss God's best, or when we feel we have failed as punishment. When we go through a challenging time or when it seems everything is going down the tubes, we may simply think we are getting what we deserve because God is mad at us. These feelings are not accurate; God does not work like that.

This event with Moses and the burning bush isn't about failure, but an encounter to experience God and allow Him to speak about going beyond. God does the same with us. He comes to us in the midst of where we are to speak to us so that His vision of us becomes our vision. Moses needs to encounter God in a way that takes him out of his defeat and into fulfilling his destiny so he can act on the things God put in his heart (Acts 7:34).

How Do We See Ourselves As God Sees Us

First of all, God puts something in our heart to do, say, or accomplish. This is seasoned in our hearts by us doing the small things over time and through what we are becoming and who we are becoming (Acts 7:22; also Psalm 22:22).

Second, we need a personal encounter. Moses needs a personal encounter with God Himself because he doesn't know Him. In response to God's directive, Moses asked who he should say was sending him (Exodus 3:13). Moses needs to experience God, our heavenly Father, and be adopted into the household of faith. He needs to know that God is **mighty to save, to deliver, and to set the captive free.**

Third, our encounter with God results in a personal relationship. Moses' encounter leads him into a friendship relationship with God as evidenced by this verse, "So the Lord spoke to Moses face to face, as a man speaks to his **friend**" (Exodus 33:11a, emphasis added). Jesus no longer calls us servants, but friends because friends know what He is doing (John 15:15). Each week, people all over the world sing this favorite hymn from their hymnals, "What a Friend We Have in Jesus;" we might need to ask ourselves if Jesus is, in fact, our friend.

Fourth, we learn to go beyond. Moses' encounter enables him to go beyond his own insecurities and lead God's people into the Promised Land. He is able to do this because he sees the desire God has placed in his heart (Acts 7:35-36) come to pass.

Finally, we need to see that God sees a much larger picture of things than we do. God uses Moses to speak prophetically about the coming of Jesus, "'The Lord God will raise up for you a Prophet like me from your brethren. Him you shall hear'" (Acts 7:37; see also Deuteronomy 18:15). God sees his people in light of eternity; however, we see ourselves in the now. As we get an accurate picture of how God sees us, we must recognize that God's field of vision spans eternity. He may be at work through us now, but the end result may not be evident for years.

Moses was able to go beyond his defeat, his discouragement, and his rejection because he refused to allow the enemy to steal his destiny. Jesus says, "The thief [the devil] does not come except to steal, and to kill and to destroy. I have come that they may have life and that they may have it more abundantly" (John 10:10). The word "abundantly" means *beyond, overflowing, superabundance, and more than enough*. Our goal should be to move forward beyond our lack, failure, and loss of significance into life more abundantly.

Pivot Points

- What seems to be a setback in the beginning, may be the steppingstone to your destiny.
- God brings us full circle to face our fears, our failures, and our being misunderstood to redeem the past and propel us into greatness.
- God's picture of our lives is greater than what we can imagine; therefore, we must see ourselves the way God sees us.
- An encounter with the Lord does more for us than anything else and changes our perspective about life and the greatness of our God.
- God's work in us is exceedingly more—beyond what we can ever think or imagine; therefore, with grateful and humble hearts, we receive His amazing grace working in our lives.

Let's pray:

Father, help me to see beyond where I cannot see and look to You, the Author and Finisher of my faith. Father, lift my eyes beyond my disappointments, frustrations, feelings of inadequacy, and fears to see the greatness of Your love for me. Father, give me eyes to see what You are doing as I look to Jesus, the Source and Finisher of my faith. Thank you for taking me from my disappointment to my destiny. Amen.

LET'S TALK ABOUT IT

Why is it important for God to give Moses a new frame of reference—a new way of looking at things—before going forward?

Why does Moses find it so difficult to go beyond his past in order to follow God's call upon his life?

What keeps us from going beyond our failures, weaknesses, or mistakes? How is God calling you to go beyond what you feel was a failure or a setback?

Why is it important to know our identity in Christ which empowers us to go beyond our setbacks to walking in the promises of God?

Why is it important for Moses to draw near to this burning bush? What happens when we draw near to God?

Which one of the pivot points speaks to you the most?

What is one thing you will take away from this lesson?

Lesson 7

GOING BEYOND OUR SETBACKS

⌘

Going beyond our setbacks to cross over into the Promised Land, the place of divine provision, the place where we walk in the fullness of the Holy Spirit, is the place of embracing and declaring the good promises of God over our lives and the lives of others. Moses sends out twelve spies to bring back a report of the land. When the twelve return, they have a time of debriefing where they show the fruit they have brought back and describe what the land is like and who lives there. The spies exclaim, "There we saw the giants…and we were like grasshoppers in our own sight, and so we were in their sight" (Numbers 13:33). Fear grips the people.

There is nothing greater that will stop you in your tracks from going forward than fear and intimidation. It will keep you from your destiny. This report and the response of the people put the children of Israel in a forty-year holding pattern until one generation passed away and another grew up among them.

This chapter is about going beyond our doubts and fears and refusing to stop short of God's plan and call. Obedience is not for the faint-hearted, but for those who choose God's way above man's way. It is

about moving past our setbacks and trusting God when we feel that we need to have all the answers before moving forward.

Let's examine this passage of Scripture that records the report of the spies for Israel:

> Then they told him, and said: "We went to the land where you sent us. It truly flows with milk and honey, and this is its fruit. Nevertheless the people who dwell in the land are strong; the cities are fortified and very large; moreover we saw the descendants of Anak there. The Amalekites dwell in the land of the South; the Hittites, the Jebusites, and the Amorites dwell in the mountains; and the Canaanites dwell by the sea and along the banks of the Jordan." Then Caleb quieted the people before Moses, and said, "Let us go up at once and take possession, for we are well able to overcome it." But the men who had gone up with him said, "We are not able to go up against the people, for they are stronger than we." And they gave the children of Israel a bad report of the land which they had spied out, saying, "The land through which we have gone as spies is a land that devours its inhabitants, and all the people whom we saw in it are men of great stature" (Numbers 13:27-32).

What does it mean for the people of Israel to go beyond?

- It is to have a faith that prevails over all obstacles (Numbers 13:30).
- It means pressing through bad reports and not be

shaken (Numbers 13:31-33).
- It means declaring fear and intimation would not keep them from their destiny (Numbers 14:9).
- It means that common sense will not rule the day, or be the measuring stick to following God's purpose and call.

Don't get me wrong; God has given us great abilities to think, reason, and plan. However, we must be led by the Holy Spirit, who supersedes our capacities, so that we may lay hold of God's power which will take us where He wants us to go even if it goes against sound logic and common sense (Numbers 14:3).

We can walk in the Spirit of wisdom and revelation of the Father's heart to know His way that leads to an overcoming life.

What keeps the people of Israel from going beyond?

First of all, they ask "why" questions instead of "who" questions: "**Why** has the Lord brought us to this land to fall by the sword, that our wives and children should become victims? Would it not be better for us to return to Egypt?" (Numbers 14:3, emphasis added). Joshua is fully aware of who they are in God: "If the Lord delights in **us**, then He will bring **us** into this land and give it to **us**, 'a land flowing with milk and honey'" (Numbers 14:8, emphasis added). We have to move beyond asking "why" questions to knowing who we are and whose we are; this must get settled in our spirits. God wants us to know who we are in Christ: His very own sons and daughters. As we wage war in the heavenlies and the battlefield of our minds, we stand from that position as sons and daughters of God. When we walk in this revelation, we can rest in that truth and live from this side of the cross victoriously.

Second, they want to cast stones instead of becoming living stones. The Bible records, "So they said to one another, 'Let us select a leader and return to Egypt.'...And all the congregation said to stone them with stones" (Numbers 14:4, 10). The children of Israel want to stone their leaders. Peter explains how Christians don't need to throw stones but become living stones: "You also, as living stones, are being built up a spiritual house, a holy priesthood, to offer up spiritual sacrifices acceptable to God through Jesus Christ" (1 Peter 2:5). The unbelief of the children of Israel makes them unable to see beyond the bad reports of giants in the land. God laments, "'How long will these people reject [despise] Me? And how long will they not believe Me, with all the [miraculous] signs which I have performed among them?'" (Numbers 14:11).

God will ensure that they are well able to take possession of what He is calling them to do. God will not only take care of them and fight for them, but He wants them to know they are His very own people, and it is He who calls them out of slavery and defeat into the light of His destiny for their lives. It is He who invites them into a dwelling place of the God of more than enough (Ephesians 2:22). The thing that keeps us from going beyond is when we do not know who we are and whose we are. Our human nature wants to **cast** stones instead of becoming **living** stones.

We need to know what keeps us from going beyond so that we can fulfill our destiny of what we can become in Christ Jesus.

What will cause us to go beyond?

Going beyond can be enabled in a couple of ways. If we learn to persevere while staying in a place longer than we intend, we can journey beyond. If we also learn to pass the tests that God gives us when giving up would be easier. Through both persevering and passing tests, we can push through our own personal desires and comforts to go where God wants us to go. The Bible says:

> "And you shall remember that the Lord your God led you all the way these forty years in the wilderness, to humble you and test you, to know what was in your heart...that He might make you know that man shall not live by bread alone; but man lives by every word that proceeds from the mouth of the Lord" (Deuteronomy 8:2-3).

When we are in a hard place in life, God strengthens us in our inner man to stay the course as we feed upon the life-giving Word of God which enables us to walk through the fire unscathed (Isaiah 43:2). Persevering is a grace given to us by God; otherwise, it becomes a time of gritting our teeth and not experiencing many victories. Persevering is leaning into Jesus and finding our rest in Him. It is watching Him bring forth our breakthrough, and discovering, in Him, a grace that carries us along as if we are on eagle's wings (Deuteronomy 32:11).

To go beyond, we must make a good confession of our faith as did Caleb when giving his report of the Promised Land, "Then Caleb quieted the people before Moses and said, 'Let us go at once and take possession [to seize, to occupy], for we are well **able** to overcome it'" (Numbers 13:30, emphasis mine).

The word "able" means *having the capacity to prevail or succeed.* Faith does not deny the reality of difficulty; it declares the power of God to prevail in the face of the problem. Christians are encouraged to "hold fast the confession of our hope without wavering, for He who promised is faithful" (Hebrews 10:23).

To go beyond, we not only feed on the word that God has for us in the now, but we must also declare, confess, and agree with God's promise and the life-giving Word He is giving us.

There is something supernatural that happens when we say what we desire and see it come to pass. When we begin to agree with God and what He has to say about it from His Word, there is something transformational that takes place. When we open our mouths and the breath of God comes forth, we begin to speak life and breakthrough while declaring that the reign and rule of God will come into whatever it is we need. We begin to experience the power and presence of God when we agree with His Word which enables us to go beyond.

Another way to go beyond is to find a reminder of God's faithfulness along the way. As we see Joshua instructing the priests in this verse:

> "Cross over before the ark of the Lord your God into the midst of the Jordan, and each one of you **take up a stone** on his shoulder, according to the number of tribes of the children of Israel, that this may be a sign among you when your children ask in time to come saying, 'What do these stones mean to you?'" (Joshua 4:5-6, emphasis mine).

The priests were to use stones, but some things we may pick up as reminders of God's faithfulness are: His vigilance to watch over the promises in His Word to ensure that His purpose and destiny for our lives will be fulfilled, His steadfastness to do for us what we cannot do for ourselves, and His unwavering love during the hard times and times of uncertainty. These are only a few reminders that testify of God's faithfulness for us to cling to as He takes us beyond our setbacks.

A testimony is something we all have.

- It is declaring God's goodness in the midst of every trial, setback, and disappointment.
- It is telling how He makes all things work together for our good and His glory (Romans 8:28). We pick up something that is of substance that carries meaning and has impacted us greatly while declaring God's goodness and faithfulness.
- It signifies what He has imparted to us about Himself, and that builds a testimony—a legacy of the God of more than enough.

A testimony does not become a testimony until we speak out what the Lord has done for us. Otherwise, we remain silent with only a thought or an idea. Once we begin to say and declare what the Lord has done for us, others are inspired by the benefits of God's goodness and His miracle-working power. Others then become witnesses to His handiwork. Therefore, tell, witness, and become a testimony of the mighty work of God so that others can say, "*If God did that for them, then He can do this for me.*"

We can shout out the victory of our God and proclaim His goodness so that it draws others to the person of Jesus Christ, and we can all glorify the Lord.

The Lord, Our Victorious One

We are looking at the truths of going beyond and what it means in our lives. We are examining biblical characters whose response to going beyond is that they did what God asked them to do. They know debating with God over the matter did little to change His mind. Their going beyond in the face of uncertainty, challenges, and adversity led to greater encounters with the Lord, and their faith grew immensely. Joshua is a man with an intense desire for God. He follows in the footsteps of Moses and will be his successor (Numbers 27:18-20). After wandering in the desert for forty years due to their fear and their lack of faith, the people of Israel are finally at the edge of the Jordan River ready to cross over into the Promised Land. The time has come.

They are passing from one season to another as God challenges His people to move forward—to go beyond.

> And the Lord said to Moses: "Take Joshua the son of Nun with you, a man in whom is the Spirit, and lay your hand on him; set him before Eleazar the priest and before all the congregation, and inaugurate him in their sight. And you shall give some of your authority to him, that all the congregation of the children of Israel may be obedient. He shall stand before Eleazar the priest, who shall inquire before the Lord for him by the judgment of the Urim. At his word they shall go out, and at his word they shall come in, he and all the children of Israel with him—all the congregation." So Moses did as the Lord commanded him. He took Joshua and set him before Eleazar the priest and before all the congregation. And he laid his hands on him and inaugurated him, just as the Lord commanded by the hand of Moses (Numbers 27:18-23).

We know these things about Joshua. His name means, "the Lord is salvation." Joshua knows the presence of God. It is recorded: "So the Lord spoke to Moses face to face, as a man speaks to his friend, and he would return to the camp, but his servant Joshua the son of Nun, a young man, did not depart from the tabernacle" (Exodus 33:11). He has a personal experience with the power of God to overcome the enemy during war (Exodus 17:14-15), and he knows of God's promise of a land flowing with milk and honey (Numbers 14:6-9).

Joshua goes beyond the wilderness into the Promised Land.

Joshua knows that the presence of God will enable them to go beyond. In addition to remaining in the tabernacle, Joshua overflows with the Spirit of God. The Bible says, "Now Joshua the son of Nun was full of the Spirit of wisdom, for Moses had laid his hands on him" (Deuteronomy 34:9a). What would it look like for us to be people of His presence? The Psalmist describes what it would be like, "O God, you are my God; early will I seek you; my soul thirsts for you in a dry and thirsty land where there is no water" (Psalm 63:1).

This is a time of moving forward, going beyond and learning to stand where the Lord asks them. It is a challenge to go beyond after they have been in the wilderness for so long. For the people of Israel, the barrier was not the Jordan River, but their barrier is fear of the people and lack of faith. Those places where we refuse to go will either be barriers or invitations—the choice is ours. Joshua knows the presence of God is all they need, and God will provide all the rest. It all boils down to faith and going beyond.

Joshua knows that the power of God will enable him to go beyond and be victorious in life.

> But Moses' hands became heavy; so they took a stone and put it under him, and he sat on it. And Aaron and Hur supported his hands, one on one side and the other on the other side...so Joshua defeated Amalek. (Exodus 17:12-13).

King David has a desire to see the Lord on high and lifted up in the place of worship. "So I **looked** for you in the

sanctuary, to see your **power and your glory**" (Psalm 63:2, emphasis mine). In our own times of worship before the Lord, for what are we looking?

When we look to Jesus:

- We are looking to Him with anticipation; we look for Him.
- We are looking to Him with expectation in the sanctuary (places of worship and the place where we experience His presence).
- We are looking to Him to see the display of His power and glory.

Joshua has faith in God that will take the children of Israel beyond. Scripture records, "Prepare provisions for yourselves, for within three days you will cross over this Jordan, to go in to possess the land which the Lord your God is giving you to possess" (Joshua 1:11). Remember, they were not fighting for victory; they are fighting from victory—the victory is already theirs. They are to position their hearts to receive it. Joshua is able to go beyond because he abides and remains in the presence of God. Joshua is able to go beyond his disappointment of having to wait forty years to see the Promised Land. He is able to go beyond seasons of frustrations, years of delays, many setbacks, and the fear that holds the people captive all the days of their lives.

What does going beyond look like?

First of all, it is looking to Jesus. The more you keep your focus on Him the more successful you will be in going beyond as Peter says, "'Lord, if it is you, command me to come to you on the water.' So He said, 'Come.' And when Peter had come down out of the boat, he walked on the water to go to Jesus" (Matthew 14:28-29). Looking to Jesus takes us beyond our fears. The Holy Spirit will strengthen you in your inner man—the new creation He has made you to be. Let the Holy Spirit take you beyond the fears that keep you confined and that hold you down from becoming the person Jesus has destined you to be in Him.

Second, it is keeping Jesus always before us. The Psalmist observes that we can look to Him and be radiant, and our faces will not be ashamed (Psalm 34:5). Fixing our eyes on Jesus causes a shift in our thinking and believing from a sense of hopelessness to being hope-filled. We can radiate in the presence of Jesus as He lifts us from shame, defeat, and frustration to a place God's glory rising upon us (Isaiah 60:1).

Third, it is to believe God wants us to succeed—to go beyond. He does not want us to fail. The Scripture assures us that God is directing our path: "The Lord directs the steps of the godly. He delights in every detail of their lives" (Psalm 37:23, NLT). Going beyond is to believe that God works all things together for our good and His glory. One of the struggles we have is the truth and revelation that God wants us to succeed, and He equips us with everything necessary to succeed, to overcome, and to go beyond. Yes, success is in the eye of the beholder; it does not help us to compare ourselves with others. Where you need to succeed may not be the same as where someone else needs to succeed. We need to repent of thinking that we are not able, capable, or gifted. Whatever God calls us to do, He will provide all we need to succeed. Do not feel guilty when God gives us success. We acknowledge God is our source and He enables us to go beyond where we have been stopping short of experiencing His glory and the beauty of His holiness.

Pivot Points

- Stepping into our destiny means leaving the familiar and taking hold of God's purpose, destiny, and call.
- Knowing who we are in Christ enables us to see ourselves as God sees us.
- The good confession of our faith is a great weapon with which to do spiritual warfare.
- Going beyond means we have received a word from the Lord, and our obedience is the key to releasing that word.
- We must pick up things that signify God's activity in our lives, and they become markers of God's grace and power from which to live.

Let's pray:

Father, thank You for showing me how much You love me by taking me beyond my fears, my worries, and my complaining. Father, let me know the joy of Your presence that enables me to overcome every obstacle. Let me taste the victory of going beyond my setbacks to where I thought that I could never get beyond. Amen!

LET'S TALK ABOUT IT

Why must we first settle in our spirits what our identity in Christ is before we can live an overcoming life?

What are some barriers that keep us from moving forward and going beyond our fears and comfort zone?

When going beyond setbacks and discouraging words, how can we make a good confession of our faith?

What happens when we keep our eyes on Jesus while going through challenging and difficult times?

Why is a testimony so powerful?

Which one of the pivot points speaks to you the most? How and in what way?

What one thing do you take away from this lesson?

Lesson 8

GOING BEYOND IN THE FACE OF ADVERSITY

⌘

Jealousy That Leads to Madness

The favor of God rests upon David as God gives him victory again and again over the enemy, and the people begin to say that David has killed ten thousand, and Saul has killed thousands (1 Samuel 18:7-8). This is a prescription for trouble. Saul struggles with his own identity and confidence in his own calling (1 Samuel 10:22) and becomes jealous. David does not intend to compete with Saul; he seeks to honor Saul and his position as king. Yet because of Saul's jealousy and pride, he looks for ways to kill David. But, God's protective hand is upon David to ensure that he becomes king over Israel as is prophesied by Samuel.

> So David went out wherever Saul sent him, and behaved wisely. And Saul set him over the men of war, and he was accepted in the sight of all the people and also in the sight of Saul's servants. Now it had happened as they were coming home, when David was returning from the slaughter of the Philistine, that the women had come out of all the cities of Israel, singing and dancing, to meet King Saul, with tambourines, with joy, and with musical instruments. So the women sang as they danced, and

> said: "Saul has slain his thousands, And David his ten thousands." Then Saul was very angry, and the saying displeased him; and he said, "They have ascribed to David ten thousands, and to me they have ascribed only thousands. Now what more can he have but the kingdom?" So Saul eyed David from that day forward (1 Samuel 18:5-9).

We must understand God's protective hand is on us, too, as we are all destined for a throne as John declares: "[He] has made us kings and priests to His God and Father" (Revelation 1:6).

This thought is reiterated when we read the lyrics of the new song sung by the Lamb's elders "And have made us kings and priests to our God and we shall reign on the earth" (Revelation 5:10). Peter in his Epistle explains it this way, "But you are a chosen generation, a royal priesthood, a holy nation, His own special people, that you may proclaim the praises of Him who called you out of darkness into His marvelous light" (1 Peter 2:9).

This chapter is about how we, like David, are royalty destined to rule and reign with Christ now and throughout eternity. But in getting to that place, we will experience setbacks, testing, trials, and adversity. We will encounter spiritual warfare on the way to ruling and reigning with Christ. The result is more than just going through the battle and adversities; God is working something eternal within us that no one or nothing will be able to take from us.

Adversity Works for Our Good

Paul states this about adversity, "For our light affliction [pressure, oppression, stress, adversity, and feeling like we are being crushed], which is but for a moment, is working for us a far more exceeding and eternal weight of glory" (2 Corinthians 4:17). Going beyond means letting these light afflictions work for us.

To see adversity, setbacks, and pressure work for us, they must be seen in the light of God's purpose and destiny that He has for us. We begin to see adversity working for us instead of against us when we start to "count it all joy when [we] fall into various trials, knowing that the testing of [our] faith produces patience [endurance, perseverance]" (James 1:2-3). When adversity comes our way instead of getting angry, frustrated, or withdrawing into our shell—do the opposite. Do as Paul declares we are to do: "Rejoice in the Lord always. Again I will say, rejoice! Let your gentleness [graciousness or self-control] be known to all men. The Lord is at hand" (Philippians 4:4-5). When we begin to bless the Lord, the presence of God comes in like a flood (Isaiah 59:19) and enables us to overcome that which has come to discourage and defeat us. There are many ways adversity can work for our good.

First, when we begin to do the opposite of what is coming at us to distract, discourage, or defeat, we are learning to reign and rule with Christ. When we learn to conquer adversity, we become stronger. This is how we become more than conquerors through Christ Jesus (Romans 8:37). God uses everything and wastes nothing, though at times we wonder how.

God can bring something good out of the messes in which we get ourselves or the messes that others have brought upon us. **Second**, when we go through these times and seasons, we learn that the Lord "works together for good to those who love God, to those who are called according to His purpose" (Romans 8:28). It may look bad, but God will turn it around for our good.

What is God's purpose for us? God's purpose is for us to live in His highest will and to see the great achievements He works in us and through us. We are His delight, and He is totally committed to us and to His best for us; He desires nothing but the best for us. When we begin to see that God is for us, not against us, we begin to see from heaven's view: what we think is working against us is, in actuality, working for us so God's glory can be displayed in us.

The **third** truth for all these things working for us is to teach us to engage in spiritual warfare. If we are going to rule and reign with Christ now and forever, then we must learn to war against principalities and powers that seek only to kill, steal, and destroy our lives, our destiny, and God's purpose for our lives.

Destined to Overcome

We are destined for the throne because this is where Christ is seated. Paul explains, "[God] raised Christ from the dead and seated Him at His right hand in the heavenly places" (Ephesians 1:20b). This truth is applied to us when Paul declares that God "made us alive together with Christ…and raised us up together, and made us sit together in the heavenly places in Christ Jesus" (Ephesians 2:5b-6). If we are seated with Christ, then we need to learn to wage war in the heavenlies as we rule and reign with Him. We have an adversary who is out to destroy us, to cause us to miss God's best, to steal our identity (who we are) in Christ, and to encourage us to falter in the face of adversity that is thrown at us. David states it this way, "Blessed be the Lord my Rock, who trains my hands for war, and my fingers for battle" (Psalm 144:1). If satan can steal our joy and our confidence in Christ and rob us of our peace, then we are giving him more credit than is due him. We don't need to pay more attention to the problem than to the One who holds the solution to the problem.

Fighting the Good Fight of Faith

One positive outcome from adversity, setbacks, and discouraging words from others is to teach us to "fight the good fight of faith, to lay hold of eternal life and to make a good confession of our faith in the presence of many witnesses" (1 Timothy 6:12). Christ has triumphed over death and the grave and has overcome the devil by "having disarmed principalities and powers, He made a public spectacle of them, triumphing over them in it" (Colossians 2:15). The Lord has disarmed the devil for our benefit; our job is to enforce His victory through spiritual warfare.

So we must not think it unusual when all sorts of distractions, adversities, and chaos break out against you. Peter describes it as:

> Beloved, do not think it strange concerning the fiery trial which is to try you, as though some strange thing

> happened to you; but rejoice to the extent that you partake of Christ's sufferings, that when His glory is revealed, you may also be glad with exceeding joy (1 Peter 4:12-13).

Again, all that seems to be working against us is in actuality working for us to display the glory of God in us and through us.

We have powerful promises from God's Word so "strengthen the hands which hang down [discouragement, disappointment, and frustration], and the feeble knees [that get weary in the battle]" (Hebrews 12:12) and stand in the strength that Christ gives. The Psalmist David says:

> I have pursued my enemies and overtaken them; neither did I turn back again till they were destroyed. I have wounded them, so that they could not rise; they have fallen under my feet. For You have armed me with strength for the battle (Psalm 18:37-39b).

Paul states it this way, "And the God of peace will crush Satan under your feet shortly. The grace of our Lord Jesus Christ be with you" (Romans 16:20).

The NKJV Study Bible defines the word "crush" as to trample upon, break in pieces, and to bruise. Our victory is a continuation of Christ's victory when He bruised the head of the serpent at Calvary. The word "crush" points to present victories over the powers of darkness as well as to the ultimate destruction of satan's kingdom at the Second Coming of Christ."

Going beyond means we are more than conquerors through Jesus Christ because greater is He who is in us than he who is in the world (1 John 4:4).

Winning Out Over Delays

The Bible not only relates how Saul's jealousy raged with hostility, oppression, and adversity against David but also about delays that David encounters on his way to the throne to be king.

In the same way, there are things we have been praying to come to pass or those encouraging words from others about our lives that seem to get further and further away with the passing of time. It is easy to become discouraged when we have a deep knowing down in our heart that God has something for us—something more—but it has not yet come to fruition, and we are still waiting.

David must have felt that way because around 15 years old, Samuel the prophet came to anoint him as king (1 Samuel 16:13), but he did not see the fruition of that until around the age of 30 when he became king over Judah and another seven years passed before he became king over Israel (2 Samuel 2:3-4; 5:1-5). Most of us are challenged when it comes to delays especially in a world that only knows instant gratification. David learns the secret of waiting on the Lord and records his thoughts about that in the Psalms. David finds the strength he needs to wait on the Lord: "Wait [in faith] on the Lord; be of good courage, and He shall strengthen your heart" (Psalm 27:14).

Waiting gives us a sense of expectation for things to come as David reminds himself, "My soul, wait silently for God alone, for my expectation [hope] is from Him" (Psalm 62:5). In every season that we go through in life, there is a "due season." David declares, "These all wait for You, that You may give them their food in due season" (Psalm 104:27).

Due Season

Most of us get tired of waiting for our due season, that time of reward, poured out blessings, and an "open heaven" where God showers upon us His goodness, grace, generosity, and favor. It is not that there are no tests, challenges, or trials; but, it is a season when the heaviness under which we have labored is lifted, our blurred or distorted vision becomes clearer than ever before, and our sense of hopelessness has passed. Our hearts are filled with overwhelming hope and peace that we have not known in a while. This is called "due season." The due season may come following a concentrated time of prayer and pursuit of the Lord. It may happen following a time of great tragedy, loss, or testing. When we experience a setback in life, there will be a time of stepping up or beyond where we presently find ourselves; however, we will reap our rewards if we don't give up.

The most crucial time in waiting for our "due season" is the time between when a promise is given to us and the time when we see the promise come to pass. It is during the delay—the waiting—when our hands get tired of holding on. Our feet get weary of walking and not seeing an end in sight, and our will to stay the course begins to diminish and wane. But this is not the time to give up even if it would be easier to do so. It is the time to press into the Lord. The Bible says that "as many as had afflictions pressed about Him to touch Him" (Mark 3:10). We need to touch Jesus, and He needs to touch us.

We also find this "pressing" into the kingdom of God that Jesus speaks of in Luke 16:16, "The law and the prophets were until John. Since that time the kingdom of God has been preached, and everyone is pressing into it." What does it mean to *press into the kingdom of God?* It means an intense pursuit of prayer, confrontation with the demonic, expectation of the miraculous, and a burning heart for evangelism. Without these things, the kingdom of God will make very little penetration into this world. "Pressing in" means that we are broken over the things that break the heart of God, and we are relentless in our pursuit of His kingdom becoming a present reality where we are.

The Promise of Breakthrough

What is the promise to those who "press in" for their due season? Scripture tells us, "And let us not grow weary while doing good, for in **due season** we shall reap if we do not lose heart" (Galatians 6:9, emphasis added). David has no idea how long or what he would have to go through to get to his "due season." He keeps the faith, and he strengthens himself in the Lord when he becomes discouraged. He hides God's Word of promise in his heart; no one could take that from him unless he relinquishes it, gives up on it, or allows someone to steal it. The promise is to those who "do not grow weary" and those who "faint not." How can we keep from growing weary or fainting? To do this, we fix our eyes on Jesus and look away from every distraction, every destructive thought, and every discouraging word so we can keep pressing into the Author and Perfector of our faith (Hebrews 12:2). We are to guard our hearts against growing weary and losing heart. We press on past our adversities by doing these things:

1. Pass Through the Valleys

First of all, although the Psalmist states, "though I walk through the valley of the shadow of death" (Psalm 23:4a), we don't camp out and live there. We don't live in the valley of adversity, but we pass through the valley to the place of refreshing, renewing, and restoration. The Psalmist also reminds us that when we go through these dry places, we should remember:

> Blessed is the man whose strength is in You, whose heart is set on pilgrimage. As they [the downtrodden and discouraged] pass through the Valley of Baca, they make it a spring; the rain also covers it with pools [blessings]. They go from strength to strength (Psalm 84:5-7a).

The word "Baca" means *weeping* and alludes to a type of balsam plant that can survive in dry conditions. Some scholars believe that the Valley of Baca referenced in this verse may also represent the Valley of Rephaim where David inquires of the Lord whether he is to go up against the Philistines. God tells David that when he hears the sound in the mulberry trees, he should advance; David did so and drove the enemy back (2 Samuel 5:22-25). We don't stay in the valley, though we may pass through the valley.

It is not the place where we are to live. We pass through the valley of weeping and come out on the other side victorious. It is from there that God takes us from strength to strength, and we become mighty men and women for God.

2. Hold on to the Promises of God

Another way to push past adversity is by holding tightly to the Word of God for the Word of God is alive and active (Hebrews 4:12), and it is the sword of the Spirit that defends us (Ephesians 6:17). This principle of holding on to God's Word when we are in the midst of battling against weariness and defeat by looking in 2 Samuel. David's mighty men are the greatest fighters of the day and renowned for their ability to fight off hundreds of men at one time, and Eleazar is one of them. In this story, Israel is retreating, and Eleazar rises up and attacks the Philistines "until his hand was weary, and his hand stuck to the sword. The Lord brought about a great victory that day" (2 Samuel 23:10b). What was it that gave Eleazar great victory that day? He held on to his sword in the heat of the battle. This represents us when all we can do is hold on to the promise of God's Word to deliver, heal, set free the captive, and give us the victory we desire.

3. Rest in God

We see the third thing we need to go beyond adversity when Jesus says, "Come to me all who labor and are heavy laden and I will give you rest" (Matthew 11:28). One of the things we, as believers, have a hard time doing is finding our place of rest in Christ. It seems as if we can trust Jesus with where we will spend eternity but have such a difficult time trusting Him with our daily activities. We seem to trust Jesus with our spiritual life, but we think He is not good with the practical things of life; instead, we try to take care of those things by ourselves. We need to read Matthew 11:28 over and over until it gets in our hearts.

Isaiah 28:12 states, "To whom He said, 'This is the rest with which you may cause the weary to rest,' And, 'This is the refreshing'; Yet they would not hear." A strong indicator of our maturity in Christ is how much we are willing to trust in Him. The word "rest" means *a resting place, a place of stillness, and a quiet place*. It conveys the idea to settle down. The Psalmist observes, "He makes me to lie down in green pastures; He leads me beside the still waters [of rest]" (Psalm 23:2).

We overcome weariness and defeat by looking to Jesus and finding in Him our place of rest, peace, and refreshing because Jesus is faithful; He has an outstanding track record.

4. Find Our Safe Place

Finally, we go beyond adversity by making the Lord our place of habitation—our dwelling place. Isaiah records what the Lord spoke, "My people will dwell in a peaceful habitation, in secure dwellings, and in quiet resting places" (Isaiah 32:18). When we make the Lord our habitation, He is our place of safety, place of security, place of protection, and our abiding place. Jesus says, "'He who **abides** in Me, and I in him, bears much fruit, for apart from Me you can do nothing" (John 15:5b, emphasis mine). We will bear fruit when we abide in Him.

Author Corrie Ten Boom writes about our relating to God: "Don't wrestle, just nestle." Our safe place will be a place of comfort and protection. The Psalmist encourages us that, "He who dwells in the secret place of the Most High shall abide under the shadow of the Almighty" (Psalm 91:1). It is in drawing near to that secret place where we are truly able to taste and see that the Lord is good (Psalm 34:8).

One of the powerful things we can do as believers is to regularly make declarations like:

> I will say of the Lord, "He is my refuge and my fortress; my God, in Him I will trust"...Because you have made the Lord, who is my refuge, even the Most High, my dwelling place, no evil shall befall me, nor shall any plague come near my dwelling (Psalm 91:2, 9-10).

Let us make the Lord our dwelling place—our place of abiding—for we have drawn near to Him, and He will "keep [us] as the apple of [His] eye; and hide [us] under the shadow of [His] wings" (Psalm 17:8). These are the ways we can go beyond adversities that bring weariness and defeat.

> Looking unto Jesus, the author and finisher of our faith, who for the joy that was set before Him endured the cross, despising the shame, and has sat down at the right hand of the throne of God. For consider Him who endured such hostility from sinners against Himself, lest you become weary and discouraged in your souls (Hebrews 12:2-3).

Pivot Points

- We are a kingdom of priests, and we will reign and rule with Christ Jesus.
- Overcoming adversity leads to advancement in the kingdom of God.
- We will wait for our due season and war against discouragement and defeat.
- God, who calls us, will ensure that He fulfills what He has spoken over our lives.
- Pressing into God is the way of knowing the heart of God.

Let's pray:

Father, I thank You that this light and momentary adversity that I am presently going through is working for my good and for Your glory. Help me to pass through the hard places as I hold on to Your Word. Help me to enter into Your rest that I find by dwelling with You. Father, I thank You that You have called me to reign and rule with You in bringing Your Kingdom to be a present reality on earth. Amen!

LET'S TALK ABOUT IT

What does it mean for us to be destined for the throne?

For what purpose are we involved in spiritual warfare?

What does "due season" mean, and what does this say to us about our own due season?

How does adversity work for our good and take us beyond our lack to God's generosity?

According to Psalm 84:5-7, what is our promise? What does it mean to go from strength to strength?

Which one of the pivot points speaks to you the most? How and in what way?

What is one thing you can take away from this lesson?

Lesson 9

GOING BEYOND THE PIT TO PURSUING

⌘

In the Bible, we see the people of Israel are continually falling in and out of a relationship with the Lord, and there seems to be no consistency in their desire to pursue the things of God and to honor and serve Him. We find in Judges 6:1 that the Lord allows the Midianites to harass, pillage, and bring great distress upon the children of Israel when we read this verse: "Then the people of Israel did evil in the sight of the Lord. So the Lord delivered them into the hand of Midian for seven years." The point of their affliction is to bring His people back to Himself and to worship Him alone. Their adversity is not to destroy them, but to bring them to the end of themselves so they can step into their destiny for greatness. The people of God, in essence, say, "*Enough is enough*," and they "cried out to the Lord because of the Midianites" (Judges 6:7). God continues to send His prophets to speak on His behalf to the people and call them back to make a spiritual course change to get out of the pit and to remind them that the way of blessing is the way of obedience.

> And it came to pass, when the children of Israel cried out to the Lord because of the Midianites, that the Lord sent a prophet to the children of Israel, who said to them, "Thus says the Lord God of Israel: 'I brought you up from Egypt and brought you out of

> the house of bondage; and I delivered you out of the hand of the Egyptians and out of the hand of all who oppressed you, and drove them out before you and gave you their land.' Also I said to you, "I am the Lord your God; do not fear the gods of the Amorites, in whose land you dwell." But you have not obeyed My voice (Judges 6:7-10).

This chapter is about hearing God's call upon our lives and responding to that call regardless of the circumstances in which we find ourselves. The call of God will empower us to overcome obstacles, setbacks, and discouragement as we receive His perspective of His relentless love for us.

Making Spiritual Adjustments

The people of Israel want to be like all the nations around them so that they could fit into their way of thinking. Yet, the Lord was saying for them not to be conformed to this world, but be transformed by the renewing of their mind (Romans 12:2). This passage in Judges tells us we are not to open a door for the enemy to drive us off God's best for our lives. We also find from this passage that the enemy seeks to steal our hopes and joys which cause us to live a life filled with intimidation, fear, and defeat. We are to make ourselves available for God's prophetic voice to speak words that will bring a spiritual adjustment to our lives. It helps to gather around us one or two persons of spiritual maturity to speak prophetically into our lives so that we are renewed in our minds and are reminded of God's promises regarding the destiny He has for us. Though we may go through a season of sifting where God deals with our hearts, He will bring us through that time victoriously with a greater love for Him and a deeper work in our lives. During these times of testing, trials, and great stress, we are destined for greatness even though it may not look so great at that moment. God does powerful work, and we need to remember that our trouble, which is but is only for a short season won't last forever; in the meantime, it is working in us a "far more exceeding and eternal weight of glory" (2 Corinthians 4:17).

We must remind ourselves that we are destined for greatness, the throne, and to overcome.

You Can't Hide Forever

Sometimes we just want to hide when God corrects us. The Bible says the Midianites are so cruel that the Israelites flee to the mountains where they set up strongholds for themselves by hiding in dens and caves (Judges 6:2). When we build strongholds in our lives, it takes God's transforming power to break free and begin to walk in our destiny. To be able to walk in our destiny for greatness, we must establish the Lord as our only stronghold, our place of refuge and safety (Psalm 18:2).

Caves and dens are not natural habitats for humanity. Sometimes we can get a cave mentality where we seek to escape from fear, defeat, hopelessness, and even self-pity. We are hiding. When we live with the belief that we got the short end of the stick or we blame others for taking what is precious from us, we feel so defeated we cannot heed the call of God.

David finds himself hiding in the cave of Adullam for fear that King Saul will kill him. Then, the prophet Gad speaks words to encourage him to leave the cave: "'Do not stay in the stronghold [cave]; depart, and go to the land of Judah'" (1 Samuel 22:5). God was saying, "*It's time to leave your cave and return to God's purpose, plan, and call.*"

Destined for Greatness

Stepping into our greatness means leaving the cave mentality behind. It means believing God's Word of promise, destiny, and hope for that is where we receive our strength to step into our destiny of greatness. The name of "Midian" means *a place of striving*. God brings us to those places of striving so that we will enter into His rest. When the children of Israel stop striving and call upon the Lord, they enter into God's rest. During this time they listen to the words of the prophet as God raises up one of the most unlikely people to lead them to victory, overcoming, and deliverance. His name is Gideon, and he is destined for greatness, even though he struggles to see himself as God sees him. Then Gideon has an encounter with God that changes everything: how God sees him, how he sees himself, and how he believes God will do something powerful through him. Through this, he steps into his destiny of greatness.

Receiving God's Perspective

Gideon is hiding by threshing wheat in the winepress hoping no one will find him. This is an unusual place for threshing wheat; it usually takes place out in the open because it is a dusty job. Gideon is hiding because he does not want what little he has to be taken from him. However, while threshing wheat, Gideon has an angelic visitation, and the angel declares to him, "'The Lord is with you, you mighty man of valor'" (Judges 6:12b). I am sure that unassuming Gideon is looking all around to see to whom this messenger is speaking. He probably thinks there must be someone else in this pit with him.

At this point, Gideon is so frustrated at his plight that he and his people find themselves in and the conditions in which they are living that he cannot believe the angel's greeting. His litany of excuses is recorded:

> Gideon said to Him, "O my lord, if the Lord is with us, why then has all this happened to us? And where are all His miracles which our fathers told us about, saying, 'Did not the Lord bring us up from Egypt?' But now the Lord has forsaken us and delivered us into the hands of the Midianites."...So he said to Him, "O my Lord, how can I save Israel? Indeed my clan is the weakest in Manasseh, and I am the least in my father's house" (Judges 6:13, 15).

When we are discouraged, frustrated, and angry, we may feel the least qualified to do anything noteworthy for the Lord, and we have a long list of why we can't do what God says we can do. Yet, between verses 13 and 15 where Gideon lists his excuses are these words, "Then the Lord turned to him and said, 'Go with the strength you have and rescue Israel from the Midianites. I am sending you!'" (Judges 6:14, NLT).

Turning from defeat and living in the pit to stepping into greatness begins when we change our viewpoint—how we go from seeing things from our perspective to see from

God's perspective. This comes from encountering His presence and receiving His words of hope, promise, and calling.

God sees us as He wants us to become. Paul speaks to Timothy that he is to stir up the gifts in him (2 Timothy 1:6). There are gifts, abilities, and talents latent within us that are buried beneath defeat, frustration, and discouragement. However, God speaks to us and says there is strength within us; He says, *"Begin to exercise that strength, for I am commissioning you for an assignment."*

Gideon must believe that God strengthens those He calls and commissions. We see this promise in Paul's prayer, "I pray that from his glorious, unlimited resources he will empower you with inner strength through his Spirit" (Ephesians 3:16, NLT). Gideon has to trust in the promise of God's abiding presence because He promises: "Surely I will be with you, and you shall defeat the Midianites as one man" (Judges 6:16). Gideon comes around to receive how God sees him when the angel refers to him as a "mighty man of valor" (Judges 6:12). The NLT records it this way, "'Mighty hero, the Lord is with you!'" The amazing thing about this statement is that God declares this over Gideon while he is still hiding in the winepress.

God sees greatness in Gideon and calls it out of him when he cannot see it himself, nor can anyone else. This greatness comes from the inside out after receiving the revelation of the Father's heart, "Eye has not seen, nor ear heard, nor have entered into the heart of man the things which God has prepared for those who love Him" (1 Corinthians 2:9). God has prepared us for greatness because of our love for Him. God takes us out of those things that confine us, enslave us, and defeat us as we set our hearts to seek Him, and from that, He prepares us for great things that honor and glorify His name. God calls Gideon while he is in the pit, but He refuses to let him remain there because His call on Gideon's life is greater than that. God always calls us from where we are to take us to where He wants us to be. He delivers us from the things that restrict and enslave us. He brings us out to show us His glory shining through us.

To each of us God, calls us a mighty man or woman of God and says, *"Arise and I will show you the greatness for which I have created you, called you, and destined you."*

Stepping into Greatness

> Then he [Gideon] said to Him, "If now I have found favor in Your sight, then show me a sign that it is You who talk with me. Do not depart from here, I pray, until I come to You and bring out my offering and set it before You." And He said, "I will wait until you come back." So Gideon went in and prepared a young goat, and unleavened bread from an ephah of flour. The meat he put in a basket, and he put the broth in a pot; and he brought them out to Him under the terebinth tree and presented them." The Angel of God said to him, "Take the meat and the unleavened bread and lay them on this rock, and pour out the broth." And he did so. Then the Angel of the LORD put out the end of the staff that was in His hand, and touched the meat and the unleavened bread; and fire rose out of the rock and consumed the meat and the unleavened bread. And the Angel of the LORD departed out of his sight. Now Gideon

> perceived that He was the Angel of the Lord. So Gideon said, "Alas, O LORD God! For I have seen the Angel of the Lord face to face (Judges 6:17-22).

To begin walking in our destiny for greatness, we must have a personal encounter with the Lord that transforms the way we see God, the way He sees us, and that changes the way we look at things from His perspective. Gideon does what any of us would do; by presenting an offering, he tries to create something that would please the Lord even though the angel did not ask Gideon to do anything, but merely receive the mandate, commission, and call that God has for him.

It seems we think we have to make ourselves acceptable before the Lord when He already accepts us in Christ. Paul describes this, "To the praise of the glory of His grace, by which He made us accepted in the Beloved" (Ephesians 1:6). The word "accepted" means *grace and more grace*. It speaks of abounding in God's grace. It is this grace that equips, enables, and empowers us to walk in our destiny for greatness. When walking in our own strength, we present what we have created as Gideon did when he said, "Do not depart from here, I pray, until I come to You and bring out my offering and set it before you" (Judges 6:18). However, Gideon's sacrifice is burned up like "hay, wood, and straw" (1 Corinthians 3:12). In the midst of this encounter, Gideon discovers the Lord as his peace (*Jehovah Shalom*) (Judges 6:24). Gideon is to no longer live in fear, defeat, and hopelessness for he is now entering into a relationship with *Abba* Father. For the first time in his life, he is experiencing wholeness, prosperity, peace, and friendship with God. The Father desires that we all know and encounter Him as the Lord, our peace, so that no matter what He is calling us to do, our uncertainty of how things are going to work out, and our feelings of being incapable of doing what He asks, we can still find peace in Him.

Building Altars

The assignment seems overwhelming, intimating, and scary as the Lord instructs Gideon to tear down the altar of Baal and cut down the wooden image beside the altar.

> Now it came to pass the same night that the Lord said to him, "Take your father's young bull, the second bull of seven years old, and tear down the altar of Baal that your father has, and cut down the wooden image that is beside it; and build an altar to the Lord your God on top of this rock in the proper arrangement, and take the second bull and offer a burnt sacrifice with the wood of the image which you shall cut down." So Gideon took ten men from among his servants and did as the Lord had said to him. But because he feared his father's household and the men of the city too much to do it by day, he did it by night (Judges 6:25-27).

Stepping into our destiny for greatness is learning to build altars along the way which builds a history with the Lord leading from one encounter to another whereby discovering God's faithfulness at every turn. We are led by His peace even though what He asks us to do may seem overwhelming. He will equip us for the task regardless of where He calls us or what He calls us to do. It does not mean that we will never be afraid or that we will not need the support and encouragement of others to witness God's mighty work in us and through us; however, God's peace will get us through. The Lord spoke through the angel to Gideon, "Peace be with you; do not fear, you shall not die" (Judges 6:23).

Building an altar to God simply means that we are growing in our trust for the Lord and finding Him to be absolutely trustworthy. We are at peace about that. The Lord takes us from victory to victory (even small ones) to change our mental and spiritual state from living in the pit, caves, dens, and strongholds to a place where we build an altar to the Lord and offer ourselves as living sacrifices (Romans 12:1).

Pulling Down Strongholds

Before an altar to the Lord can be established as a place of encountering His presence, strongholds must be pulled down and replaced. These strongholds are the things that prevent us from stepping into our destiny for greatness.

We take ground from the enemy little by little until the things to which we have looked are torn down and replaced with the "Lord-is-our-Peace" (Judges 6:24). Staying the course in the midst of adversity builds the necessary spiritual character that equips us to walk into our destiny for greatness. God wants to do something great and unique in you and through you where our only thought is: this is God!

The word gets out that Gideon and his friends have pulled down the stronghold of Baal's altar and replaced it with an altar to the Lord. The men of the city were upset, but Gideon's father, Joash, comes to his rescue and challenges the men's thinking: "If he is a god [Baal], let him plead for himself, because his altar has been torn down!" (Judges

6:31b). Baal never responds because he is a creation of man and not God, so the case is closed. Through pulling down strongholds at the instruction of the Lord, Gideon moves yet closer to stepping into greatness.

Possessed by the Spirit

One of the most amazing verses of Scripture is found in Judges 6:34, "But the Spirit of the Lord came upon Gideon; then he blew the trumpet, and the Abiezrites gathered behind him." The NLT translates it this way, "Then the Spirit of the Lord took possession of Gideon." The word "possession" means to "take control" or "wrap around." From the Hebrew, this verse literally means that the Holy Spirit clothes Himself with Gideon. In the New Testament, the apostle Paul teaches that our inner strength comes through His Spirit (Ephesians 3:16, NLT).

Stepping into our destiny of greatness can never come to pass apart from the work and power of the Holy Spirit. This "possession" was the launching pad for Gideon and his assignment to lead the people of Israel from a spirit of poverty to a spirit of prevailing, triumph, and overcoming. Gideon's perspective of himself and who God is and what He is able to do changes dramatically. When we are clothed in the Holy Spirit, we can receive the Spirit's direction and leadership, and we become the kind of army that God is looking for to war and overcome the enemy as we can see in the Scripture passage below:

> Now therefore, proclaim in the hearing of the people, saying, "Whoever is fearful and afraid, let him turn and depart at once from Mount Gilead." And twenty-two thousand of the people returned,

> and ten thousand remained. But the Lord said to Gideon, "The people are still too many; bring them down to the water, and I will test them for you there." Then it will be, that of whom I say to you, "This one shall go with you," the same shall go with you; and of whomever I say to you, "This one shall not go with you," the same shall not go. So he brought the people down to the water. And the Lord said to Gideon, "Everyone who laps from the water with his tongue, as a dog laps, you shall set apart by himself; likewise everyone who gets down on his knees to drink." And the number of those who lapped, putting their hand to their mouth, was three hundred men; but all the rest of the people got down on their knees to drink water. Then the Lord said to Gideon, "By the three hundred men who lapped I will save you, and deliver the Midianites into your hand. Let all the other people go, every man to his place" (Judges 7:3-7).

The great challenge Gideon faces is to reduce the army to the point where the people know it is not by might, nor by power, but by the Spirit of the Lord (Zechariah 4:6). It is to be understood that our dependence is entirely upon Him and unless He does it, it won't get done. As we cooperate with the Holy Spirit, we fight not from our might and strength but through God's mighty power working through us. Thereby, the Spirit of the living God possesses us for the work at hand.

God's way may seem a bit odd and unpredictable when it comes to putting together His army, but we must understand this:

> The weapons of our warfare are not carnal [of the flesh] but mighty in God for pulling down strongholds, casting down arguments and every high thing that exalts itself against the knowledge of God, bringing every thought into captivity to the obedience of Christ" (2 Corinthians 10:4-5).

In this story, we have an orderly account of how God puts His army together. Those who are fearful, anxious, and doubtful are released and sent home. We see that God may say the army is still too large because if you win the battle, you will brag about your conquest. Therefore, let's see who keeps watch while drinking from the river for these are the ones who are ready for battle and have their eyes on the enemy. They are not caught off guard, but well prepared for the Lord's battle. Keeping watch is a mindset of preparedness and readiness; these warriors have a realization of the need for sober thinking and right believing.

The Witness of the Spirit

The Lord helps Gideon put together His army to take back what the enemy has stolen and to end the oppression under which the people of Israel have been living. They are declaring: this day we fight. Gideon needs the assurance that this is of God and that He will deliver them from their enemies. To eliminate Gideon's fear, the Lord instructs him to go down into the camp of the enemy to hear the report of the Lord.

> It happened on the same night that the Lord said to him, "Arise, go down against the camp, for I have delivered it into your hand. But if you are afraid to go

> down, go down to the camp with Purah your servant, and you shall hear what they say; and afterward your hands shall be strengthened to go down against the camp." Then he went down with Purah his servant to the outpost of the armed men who were in the camp. Now the Midianites and Amalekites, all the people of the East, were lying in the valley as numerous as locusts; and their camels were without number, as the sand by the seashore in multitude. And when Gideon had come, there was a man telling a dream to his companion. He said, "I have had a dream: To my surprise, a loaf of barley bread tumbled into the camp of Midian; it came to a tent and struck it so that it fell and overturned, and the tent collapsed." Then his companion answered and said, "This is nothing else but the sword of Gideon the son of Joash, a man of Israel! Into his hand God has delivered Midian and the whole camp." And so it was, when Gideon heard the telling of the dream and its interpretation, that he worshiped. He returned to the camp of Israel, and said, "Arise, for the Lord has delivered the camp of Midian into your hand" (Judges 7:13-15).

God gives a dream to the enemy about the surety of Gideon's victory. Gideon breaks into worship for all of God's goodness and the hope and promise He has given to them. The only thing Gideon can do at this point is to give praise and worship to the King of Kings and Lord of Lords. Upon hearing the dream and its interpretation, he is so encouraged that he goes back to the three hundred and declares, "'Arise, for the Lord has delivered the camp of Midian into your hand'" (Judges 7:15b). Gideon's mentality immediately goes from victim to victor as his faith increases.

> The church will never win wars with a cruise ship mentality! Churches should be battleships where everyone is on call, where everyone has a responsibility and where everyone is trying to make a difference. To win the spiritual battles a church faces, everyone must be involved.
>
> —Cordeiro and Lewis, ***Culture Shift***[8]

The three hundred men divide into three companies and Gideon "put[s] a trumpet into every man's hand, with empty pitchers, and torches inside the pitchers" (Judges 7:16b). The trumpet represents the breath of God that fills each man's mouth. It becomes the instrument through which He sounds forth the defeat of the enemy and victory for the people of God. The torches represent the light of God that would come upon them as Isaiah declares: "Arise, shine; for your light has come! And the glory of the Lord is risen upon you" (Isaiah 60:1). Paul declares the power of the light of Christ, "For it is God who commanded light to shine out of darkness, who has shone in our hearts to give the light of the knowledge of the glory of God in the face of Jesus Christ" (2 Corinthians 4:6).

The Sword of the Spirit is the Word of God

As the leader of the men who would stand in the gap for the people of God, Gideon receives further instructions concerning the trumpets, the pitchers and torches when they are given the words to shout: "The sword of the Lord and of Gideon!" (Judges 7:18b). Gideon steps into his destiny for greatness, not for his great exploits nor the boldness he shows in times of trials, but for standing on God's behalf through it all. The key to Gideon moving into his destiny is being filled with the Holy Spirit and power to do only what God enables him to do. He is wrapped and encompassed by the Spirit of the Lord.

This is the key for us also to step into our destiny for greatness—being possessed by the Spirit of the Lord.

As the men lift their swords, high in the light of their Redeemer, they declare their victory. God confuses the enemy, and they run for their lives. However, Gideon's men are relentless in their desire to rid the enemy from ever robbing, destroying, and oppressing again. God delivers the enemy into the hands of Gideon and his army when they are "exhausted, but still in pursuit" (Judges 8:4).

Gideon goes from hiding in the pit of the winepress to being a victor. Gideon is the least likely person to step into his destiny for greatness because of how he feels about himself, the plight in which he found himself, and the hopelessness of ever seeing change take place. He has relegated himself to living below his calling and his destiny. But, God takes the least likely and turns them into warriors—into champions. They will be men and women who pursue God and become so full of Him that their quest for more leaves His praise always on their lips. Our pursuit of God should be relentless so that we will not settle for less than God's best in our lives and the lives of others. These are the ones who go beyond into their destiny for greatness.

Pivot Points

- God calls us beyond the "cave" or "pit" mentality to living in the abundance of His grace.
- We are destined for greatness through a personal encounter with Jesus Christ.
- God intends that we live as overcomers in this life through the power of the Holy Spirit (1 John 4:4). We are more than conquerors through Jesus Christ.
- Hearing and heeding God's call upon our lives is fulfilling our spiritual destiny.
- Let us submit ourselves to Christ and be possessed by the Holy Spirit as we experience His presence around us.

Our prayer is:

Father, I thank You that when You see me in the midst of overwhelming circumstances, You provide a way out for me. Thank You that it is Your intention to make me an overcomer in this life. Father, I thank You for the destiny, purpose, and calling that You have upon my life and that I can quit striving to make it. I declare that I am going from being in the pit of adversity to pursuing you with all my might. Thank you for my place of rest and peace in You. Amen!

LET'S TALK ABOUT IT

What can cause us to have a cave mentality and live from that perspective?

What keeps Gideon from stepping into his destiny for greatness? What prevents us from stepping into our destiny for greatness?

What does it mean to be possessed by the Holy Spirit?

How can we allow the Holy Spirit to take possession of us? In what way can we give the Holy Spirit full access to our lives?

Why must we get God's perspective about our lives to see what He is doing in us and through us, and to go beyond our present circumstances?

Why does God want to give us victory over those areas in which we find ourselves striving?

Which one of the pivot points speaks to you the most? How and in what way?

What is one thing you can take away from this lesson?

Lesson 10

GOING BEYOND—WHEN GOD MAKES A WAY

⌘

There is power in retelling the story of how God makes a way when there seems to be no way. In all places of life, whether good times or tough times, we need to hear the stories again and again that give us hope, promise, and victory. We need to be reminded of whose we are and that God is God; there is none like Him. Testify to the fact that the One who saves us is also the One who keeps us and delivers us. In the same manner, let's explore when Luke reminds us of the time when Paul and two hundred and seventy-six people on board a ship sailing to Rome encounter a great storm at sea that threatens to destroy the ship and all those who are on it.

This chapter is about how God saves, delivers, and speaks words of hope and promise to those who are caught in the violent storms of life. God makes a way because He is the Way-Maker. He is the One who takes us beyond the storms. When life is at its lowest and bleakest, God is about to work in an extraordinary way that demonstrates His glory, His power, and His presence.

God is the Way-Maker in the Midst of the Storm

On the third day we threw the ship's tackle overboard with our own hands. Now when neither sun nor stars appeared for many days, and no small tempest beat on us, all hope that we would be saved was finally given up. But after long abstinence from food, then Paul stood in the midst of them and said, "Men, you should have listened to me, and not have sailed from Crete and incurred this disaster and loss. And now I urge you to take heart, for there will be no loss of life among you, but only of the ship. For there stood by me this night an angel of the God to whom I belong and whom I serve, saying, 'Do not be afraid, Paul; you must be brought before Caesar; and indeed God has granted you all those who sail with you.' Therefore take heart, men, for I believe God that it will be just as it was told me. However, we must run aground on a certain island... And as day was about to dawn, Paul implored them all to take food, saying, "Today is the fourteenth day you have waited and continued without food, and eaten nothing. Therefore I urge you to take nourishment, for this is for your survival, since not a hair will fall from the head of any of you." And when he had said these things, he took bread and gave thanks to God in the presence of them all; and when he had broken it he began to eat. Then they were all encouraged, and also took food themselves. And in all we were two hundred and seventy-six persons on the ship. So when they had eaten enough, they lightened the ship and threw out the wheat into the sea (Acts 27:19-26, 33-38).

First of all, through the storms of life, we find that God is strong enough. When the storm winds blow, we find that our future looks bleak and our faith tested, our response may be like those who are caught in this storm. We see the crew's state of mind: "All hope that we would be saved was finally given up" (Acts 27:20b). They lighten the load; they do all they can, and still, all hope of surviving the storm is lost. Coming to the end of themselves, they hope for the best. Our response to times like this is that the God who saves us is also well-able to rescue and deliver us.

In the Old Testament, King Jehoshaphat and the people of Judah are facing their own storm when the enemy nations come against them. The people look to God and say, "'O our God, will You not judge them [the enemy nations]? For we have no power against this great multitude that is coming against us; nor do we know what to do, but our eyes are upon You'" (2 Chronicles 20:12). When it seems as if all hope is gone, that is when God intervenes. When we place our eyes upon Him, we are open to hearing what He has to say to us in the midst of the storm and hearing a word of hope and promise for our future. The best place we can ever be is where we have to depend totally on the Lord because that is the place where He does His greatest work and displays His mighty power. In our weakness, He demonstrates His strength.

Second, God's assurance is faithful during those stormy times. When at the point of crisis, God has something to say to those on board the ship as Paul declares:

> "And now I urge you to take heart [courage], for there will be no loss of life among you, but only of

> the ship. For there stood by me this night an angel of the God to whom I belong and whom I serve, saying, 'Do not be afraid…and indeed God has granted you all those who sail with you.' Therefore take heart, men, for I believe God that it will be just as it was told me" (Acts 27:22-25).

The word "granted" comes from the root word meaning *grace or favor has been shown*. When we are facing storms of life and challenging days and the enemies of fear, defeat, and discouragement are nipping at our heels, we are suddenly open to hear and ready to receive what God is saying to us about overcoming the adversities we face.

In the book of 2 Chronicles, God has a word for Jehoshaphat and the people of Israel when facing the enemy nations that we can take to heart. The Spirit of the Lord comes upon Jahaziel and says:

> "'Do not be afraid nor dismayed because of this great multitude, for the battle is not yours, but God's... You will not need to fight in this battle. Position yourselves, stand still and see the salvation of the Lord, who is with you'" (2 Chronicles 20:15b, 17a).

When we feel the most vulnerable with all sorts of fears attacking us, and we become desperate for a breakthrough, God steps in to demonstrate His power. He works on our behalf to assure us of His presence and His ability to rescue us because we are His sons and daughters filled with purpose and promise.

Finally, a great testimony is often birthed during a great storm. The great test of facing the storms at sea, receiving the encouraging Word of the Lord, and believing His Word leads to a great ministry opportunity to the people of Malta.

- They are welcomed and treated kindly by the people (Acts 28:1-2).
- God uses a snakebite to open the door for Paul to pray for the father of Malta's leaders (Acts 28:7-8).
- This healing demonstration of the love and grace of God lead to even more opportunities for ministry and prayer (Acts 28:9-10).

Like Paul, when God takes us through the storms, we become witnesses and give testimony of His grace, His power to save, and His ability to deliver us from that which would seek to discourage us. God takes us beyond where we cannot go on our own to the place He has planned for us to demonstrate His power and glory.

Jehoshaphat and the people of Judah discover this to be true. Scripture says, "Then they returned, every man of Judah and Jerusalem, with Jehoshaphat in front of them, to go back to Jerusalem with joy, for the Lord had made them rejoice over their enemies" (2 Chronicles 20:27). When we fix our eyes on the Lord and gladly receive the word of direction that He has for us while standing in faith to see what the Lord will do, rejoicing will come.

God is our Way-Maker when there seems to be no way. Not only does he make a way, but He makes us triumphant. When we pass through the storms, we can look to Him, receive from Him, and stand upon the Word of promise that He gives to us. Paul describes it this way, "Yet in all these things we are more than conquerors through Him who loved us" (Romans 8:37).

God is the Way-Maker through the Deep Waters

Isaiah reminds God's people of who they are and what He will do for them in the midst of crisis, in the midst of hard times, and in the midst of challenging days:

> Thus says the Lord, who makes a way in the sea and a path through the mighty waters, who brings forth the chariot and horse, the army and the power (They shall lie down together, they shall not rise; they are extinguished, they are quenched like a wick): "Do not remember the former things, nor consider the things of old. Behold, I will do a new thing, now it shall spring forth; shall you not know it? I will even make a road in the wilderness and rivers in the desert. The beast of the field will honor Me, the jackals and the ostriches, because I give waters in the wilderness and rivers in the desert, to give drink to My people, My chosen. This people I have formed for Myself; they shall declare My praise (Isaiah 43:16-21).

We must rehearse our victories that are given by God's mighty hand, and we need to be mindful of where He is taking us. Isaiah references the crossing of the Red Sea when he retells the story of how God made a way for His people when it seems the end had come, but God "makes a way in the sea and a path through the mighty waters" (v. 16). Let's look at the crossing of the Red Sea as it unfolds in Exodus 14:10-16 where we can glean these truths:

- Their greatest fears are catching up with them. "So they were very afraid, and the children of Israel cried out to the Lord" (Exodus 14:10b).
- Their greatest regret is following after Moses. "'Because there were no graves in Egypt, have you taken us away to die in the wilderness?'" (Exodus 14:11).
- Their greatest need is to look to the Savior. "'Do not be afraid. Stand still, and see the salvation of the Lord, which He will accomplish for you today'" (Exodus 14:13).
- Their greatest days are ahead of them. We all must be reminded that when things seem to be the bleakest, breakthrough is just around the corner. "'Tell the children of Israel to go forward'" (Exodus 14:15).

The Psalmist also reminds himself of God's mighty works: "Your way was in the sea, Your path in the great waters, and Your footsteps were not known" (Psalm 77:19). In other words, God is taking them where they have never been before; He is taking them beyond their fears, doubts, and disobedience to a place of safety, shelter, and abiding. Encourage one another—encourage yourselves—with testimonies of God's faithfulness to deliver. We need to be reminded that the One who saves us is also the One who delivers and keeps us.

God is the Way-Maker through the Fiery Furnace

King Nebuchadnezzar takes Daniel and his three companions captive; they make a great impression on him and actually find favor in his sight which gives them places of prominence and leadership. However, when everyone is commanded to bow and worship a statue of the king, Shadrach, Meshach, and Abed-Nego refuse. The king gets angry and commands they be thrown into the fiery furnace and consumed. When we look at the life of Daniel, we see how God makes a way for us.

Four truths of how God makes a way in the fiery furnace:

The **first** truth is that the captives declare their faith before the king when they say, "'Our God whom we serve is **able to deliver** us from the burning fiery furnace, and **He will deliver** us from your hand, O king'" (Daniel 3:17, emphasis added). When it seems as if it is all over and there is no way of escape, God comes to our aid and delivers us from that which may destroy us. Paul declares about the Lord, "Who **delivered** us from so great a death, and **does deliver** us; in whom we trust that He will **still deliver** us" (2 Corinthians 1:10, emphasis added).

There are times and places where we just make our stand against all odds. When every cell in our body shouts, "*Give in and give up*," we choose to stand and believe God. We make a declaration about our faith in God that He is more than enough in every situation, every challenge, and every adversity we face in life. At some point, the Spirit of God rises up within us, and we declare what Martin Luther said in 1521, "Here I stand; I can do no other. God help me."

David declares, "He who dwells in the secret place of the Most High, shall abide under the shadow of the Almighty" (Psalm 91:1). "Almighty" means *the all-sufficient God who is eternally capable of being all that His people need*. When was there a time you simply had to stand and declare your faith in the midst of uncertain and challenging times?

The **second** truth we can see about being in the fiery furnace is that they surrender themselves totally to the One who saves, delivers, and releases them:

> "**But if not**, let it be known to you, O king, that we do not serve your gods, nor will we worship the gold image which you have set up…And he commanded certain mighty men of valor who were in his army to bind Shadrach, Meshach and Abed-Nego, and cast them into the burning fiery furnace" (Daniel 3:18, 20; emphasis added).

There is always a cost to discipleship. There is always a consequence of following Jesus with all your heart. There is a price to be paid in declaring the lordship of Jesus in all things and not succumb to the naysayers, critics, and pessimists who always see the worst, believe the worst, and speak the worst. Yet, Isaiah has words of great hope and promise when he records God saying, "When you walk through the fire, you shall not be burned, nor shall the flame scorch you. For I am the Lord your God, the Holy One of Israel, your Savior" (Isaiah 43:2-3). Prayerfully, we will all come to those moments where we will declare the goodness of God and live totally surrendered to the Lordship of Jesus in our lives. We may be forsaken and we may walk alone, but we must decide to follow Him no matter the cost. A classic hymn that is sung all over the world includes this lyric, "I have decided to follow Jesus…though none go with me, still I will follow." What does it mean to you to live totally surrendered to the Lordship of Jesus in your life?

The **third** truth is that the three Hebrew children discover they were not alone in the midst of the fiery furnace:

> Then King Nebuchadnezzar was astonished; and he rose in haste and spoke, saying to his counselors, "Did we not cast three men bound into the midst of the fire?" They answered and said to the king, "True, O king." "Look!" he answered, "I see **four men loose**, walking in the midst of the fire; and they are not hurt, and the form of the fourth is like the Son of God" (Daniel 3:24-25, emphasis added).

Our take away from this truth is:

- Adversity does not have to get the best of us, because the presence of Christ in the midst of us is mighty.
- We can keep our cool in the midst of fiery adversity and testing because the God of all comfort is with us.
- The adversities and challenges that we face in life do not need to keep us bound, enslaved, or confined. In the midst of these things, we can experience the freedom, joy, and peace of God that keeps us even in the middle of our trials.

The **fourth** truth is that God delivers so we can give testimony of His greatness. We see King Nebuchadnezzar testify about the God of Shadrach, Meshach, and Abed-Nego:

> "God...delivered His servants who trusted in Him, and they have frustrated the king's word, and yielded their bodies, that they should not serve nor worship

> any god except their own God!...There is no other God who can deliver like this" (Daniel 3:28b, 29b).

These three men trust God to deliver them and make their stand against the evils of the day and declare the goodness of God among an unbelieving people. They experience deliverance and become witnesses of the mighty power of God to save. Shadrach, Meshach, and Abed-Nego are promoted, not only in the natural but also in the spiritual. They overcome adversity and testing; when their faith is challenged, they stand their ground and believe God. The Lord takes us beyond our adversity and causes us to experience Him in the midst of what we are going through. God takes us beyond all that would come against us, even when the enemy is setting us up for defeat. Our responsibility when God shows Himself powerful and mighty to deliver in a way that demonstrates His power and glory is to share His testimony and sing His praises.

What Does it Mean that Jesus is the Way-Maker?

First of all, Jesus is still making a way where there seems no way; He is the Lord "who makes a way" (Isaiah 43:16). The phrase "makes a way" is present tense, and we can have confidence that God makes a way for us today, just as He did for His people going through the Red Sea. Jesus said, "I am the **way,** the truth and the life" (John 14:6). We all face our "red seas," those places where it seems it is all over. We may be at a dead end, or our worst fears have caught up with us, but that is when God makes a way. He makes a way for His people as they come out of Egypt into the Promised Land, and He will do the same for us. God wants His people to succeed; He does not set us up for failure.

How were the Israelites instructed to pass through the storm they were facing?

- They were to have total dependence upon the Lord.
- God says, *"Watch what I will do. I will give you victory over the enemies of fear, discouragement, and defeat."*
- The Lord wants us to rest in His ability to deliver us, make a way for us, and protect us.
- The Lord wants us to move forward and avoid being stationary; we are to pursue His presence actively.

Second, Jesus is the Way-maker because He withholds nothing. God says He's at work anew as we read in the Scripture, "Behold, I will do a new thing, now it shall spring forth; shall you not know it?" (Isaiah 43:19a). God is giving us a new spirit that knows and responds to Him. He later says, "I will give you a new heart and put a new spirit within you; I will take the heart of stone [unresponsive, inflexible] out of your flesh and give you a heart of flesh [responsive, receptive]" (Ezekiel 36:26).

God withholds nothing:

- When our resources stop, God's resources never cease.
  "And my God will supply every need of yours according to his riches in glory in Christ Jesus" (Philippians 4:19, ESV).
- When our wisdom is lacking, God's wisdom is inexhaustible.
  "If you need wisdom, ask our generous God, and he will give it to you. He will not rebuke you for asking" (James 1:5, NLT).

- When our strength fails, God's strength is ever increasing.
  "He gives power to the weak, and to those who have no might He increases strength" (Isaiah 40:29).
- When our way is filled with anxiety and worry, God's peace prevails.
  "'These things I have spoken to you, that in Me you may have peace'" (John 16:33).
- When it seems we have lost our way, God brings clarity and purpose.
  "This is the way, walk in it" (Isaiah 30:21). We are to walk in the light God has given to us. It is "in Your light we see light" (Psalm 36:9).

Third, Jesus is the Way-maker because He satisfies the deepest desires of the heart. The Lord claims us as His own when He says, "Because I give waters in the wilderness and rivers in the desert, to give drink to My people, My chosen. This people I have formed for Myself; they shall declare My praise" (Isaiah 43:20b-21). This promise becomes that of all Christians when we read, "But you are a chosen generation, a royal priesthood, a holy nation, His own special people, that you may proclaim the praises of Him who called you out of darkness into His marvelous light" (1 Peter 2:9).

The Lord will take us by the hand to lead and guide us. He promises this by saying, "I will bring the blind by a way they did not know; I will lead them in paths they have not known...I will make darkness light before them" (Isaiah 42:16). As He leads us, we can trust that He will give us a peace that washes away our fears, anxieties, and doubts. Jesus promises, "'Peace I leave with you...not as the world gives, do I give to you. Let not your heart be troubled, neither let it be afraid'" (John 14:27).

God is the Way-Maker who makes a way through which we can personally encounter His presence in our lives and see Him working through us. We pray for divine encounters because the Lord reveals Himself to us individually in ways we may not have experienced before; revelation always precedes experience which leads to a testimony of God's greatness and goodness. He takes us beyond our boundaries and borders as His glory covers the earth (Habakkuk 3:3). He takes us beyond the things that restrict us and bind us to a place of freedom, joy, and expectancy. He takes us beyond our limited thinking to His unlimited thoughts as the "earth is filled with his praise" (Habakkuk 3:3b, NLT). What a wonderful God He is!

Pivot Points

- God meets us in the storms and takes us through them.
- God makes a way when there seems to be no way.
- God meets us in the furnace of trial and causes us to triumph.
- God takes us through times of adversity as we watch Him fight for us.
- God takes us through the deep waters to show us that His grace is greater than the deepest waters we may go through.

Let this be your prayer:

Father, I ask that You make a way where there seems to be no way in my own mind. Please lift my eyes from the circumstances that surround me that seem so overwhelming. Lord, thank You for the lift in life that only You can give. Take my hand and lead me in all the right paths. Father, You are the Way-Maker as I follow You in the way of blessing, provision, and breakthrough. Amen.

LET'S TALK ABOUT IT

What does it mean that God is the Way-maker?

When have you encountered the Lord as the Way-maker where it seems there was no way forward?

How does King Jehoshaphat go beyond the uncertainty they were facing?

How do Paul and his companions go beyond the storm in which they found themselves?

How do Moses and the people of God find a way beyond while being chased by the Egyptian army?

How do Shadrach, Meshach, and Abed-Nego move beyond the fiery trial in which they find themselves?

Which one of the pivot points speaks to you the most? How and in what way?

What is one thing you are going to take away from this lesson?

Lesson 11

GOING BEYOND—GOD'S LOVE IS MORE THAN ENOUGH

⌘

We have been looking at what it means to go beyond our last step. Only through Christ can God takes us beyond our setbacks, beyond our struggles, beyond our disappointments, and beyond what seems to be uncertain. God is the One who makes a way where there seems to be no way. God, our heavenly Father, has designed us for a purpose; He has begun a good work in us and is watching over that work to ensure it comes to pass (Philippians 1:6).

The next questions we will look at is: how do we respond to the breakthroughs the Lord has given to us? What do we do following the victory? How do we walk out what God has put within us? What makes our walk with Christ different from what we have just stepped out of and through (2 Corinthians 4:16-17)? How can we now be witnesses of the transformation Jesus has made in us? How can we let the light of the glory of God shine through us as we give testimony to His greatness, His power, His love, and His mighty presence in us (2 Corinthians 3:18)?

Let's take the next three chapters and discuss the answers to these questions as we demonstrate the transformed life while we co-labor with God to bring His Kingdom to bear upon the earth.

We will begin by looking in the book of Acts at those who encounter the love of Christ and what happens when they do. Saul, who became known as Paul, experiences the love of Christ on his way to Damascus to arrest Christians. Historians describe Saul as "a wild and ferocious beast" out to destroy those who were followers of the Way. On the road to Damascus, Saul has a powerful encounter with Christ that changes his life and name forever. Saul becomes Paul and the writer of two-thirds of the New Testament. We don't have to have a Paul experience to be a follower of Jesus; our encounter with Christ may be quiet, but powerful. These verses describe his encounter:

> Then Saul, still breathing threats and murder against the disciples of the Lord, went to the high priest and asked letters from him to the synagogues of Damascus, so that if he found any who were of the Way, whether men or women, he might bring them bound to Jerusalem. As he journeyed he came near Damascus, and suddenly a light shone around him from heaven. Then he fell to the ground, and heard a voice saying to him, "Saul, Saul, why are you persecuting Me?" And he said, "Who are You, Lord?" Then the Lord said, "I am Jesus, whom you are persecuting. It is hard for you to kick against the goads." So he, trembling and astonished, said, "Lord, what do You want me to do?" Then the Lord said to him, "Arise and go into the city, and you will be told what you must do." And the men who journeyed with him stood speechless, hearing a voice but seeing no one. Then Saul arose from the ground, and when his eyes were opened he saw no one. But they led him by the hand and brought him into Damascus.

> And he was three days without sight, and neither ate nor drank (Acts 9:1-9).

Paul's Encounter With the Love of Christ

We find that God comes to Paul in such a way that could not be ignored. Here is his account:

> "At midday, O king, along the road I saw a light from heaven, brighter than the sun, shining around me and those who journeyed with me. And when we all had fallen to the ground, I heard a voice speaking to me" (Acts 26:13-14a).

Paul's conversion consists of supernatural light, a vision, falling under the power of God, and hearing the voice of God. Paul describes this light in his second letter to the Corinthians: "For it is God who commanded light to shine out of darkness, who has shone in our hearts to give the light of the knowledge of the glory of God in the face of Jesus Christ" (2 Corinthians 4:6).

The one who is struck blind by the light of Christ is the one who brings light to those who are in spiritual darkness. Jesus describes Paul's call as being "to open their eyes, in order to turn them from darkness to light, and from the power of Satan to God, that they may receive forgiveness of sins and an inheritance among those who are sanctified by faith in Me'" (Acts 26:18).

In Romans 5:5, Paul tells us that the love of Christ is poured out into our hearts by the Holy Spirit. So we see Ananias introducing Saul to the love of God when he says, "'Brother Saul, the Lord Jesus, who appeared to you on the road as you came, has sent me that you may receive your sight and be filled with the Holy Spirit'" (Acts 9:17).

We learn essential truths from Paul's encounter with the love of Christ:

First of all, God's love brings Him to us at the most unexpected times and in the most unexpected ways. We can see this in how Saul encounters God; it was the farthest thing from his mind to meet Him on the road to Damascus. When we least expect to see God show up, He shows up and makes Himself known to us. Other instances of God unexpectedly showing up is when the angel surprises Mary and says that she will give birth to the Son of God. When Zacharias is not looking for God, He shows up and says that they will have a son in their old age and call him John the Baptist. Jesus shows up to Peter and John and makes this offer: "Follow Me and I will make you fishers of men" (Matthew 4:19). God comes in His love to make Himself known to us, to give us a testimony of His goodness, and to demonstrate His love for us.

Second, God gives each one of us the message of Good News to share with others. For Paul, his message is to bring the light of the gospel in the person of Jesus Christ to the Gentiles. The result is God taking him on missionary journeys to places where the gospel has yet to be preached. God gives each of us a call to follow Him and to share with others the message He has given us. We see that our testimony should always point to God when Paul writes, "But we have this treasure in earthen vessels, that the excellence of the power may be of God and not of us" (2 Corinthians 4:7).

Third, we find obedience to His love is required for the plan, purpose, and call of God to be fulfilled. Love commands our obedience which will vary according to God's purpose and plan for our lives. Paul says to King Agrippa, "I was not disobedient to the heavenly vision, but declared first to those in Damascus and in Jerusalem, and throughout all the region of Judea, and then to the Gentiles, that they should repent, turn to God and do works befitting repentance" (Acts 26:19-20). Let us be able to say with conviction: *we have followed and obeyed the Lord to the best of our understanding."*

Ananias: Obedience is the Key to Overcoming

Ananias is an example of a reluctant disciple. However, he is willing to co-labor with Christ's love in a mission that leads to the transformation of one who would have a profound impact upon Christian life, namely the apostle Paul (Acts 9:15-16). God can use any and all of us as we make ourselves available to Him, even if we are a bit shy or reluctant. The following passage describes Ananias and how he feels when God calls him to go beyond his fears, reluctance, and uncertainty to pray for someone whose agenda is to put into prison those who believe in Jesus Christ.

> Now there was a certain disciple at Damascus named Ananias; and to him the Lord said in a vision, "Ananias." And he said, "Here I am, Lord." So the Lord said to him, "Arise and go to the street called Straight, and inquire at the house of Judas for one called Saul of Tarsus, for behold, he is praying. And in a vision he has seen a man named Ananias coming in and putting his hand on him, so that he might receive

> his sight." Then Ananias answered, "Lord, I have heard from many about this man, how much harm he has done to Your saints in Jerusalem. And here he has authority from the chief priests to bind all who call on Your name." But the Lord said to him, "Go, for he is a chosen vessel of Mine to bear My name before Gentiles, kings, and the children of Israel. For I will show him how many things he must suffer for My name's sake." And Ananias went his way and entered the house; and laying his hands on him he said, "Brother Saul, the Lord Jesus, who appeared to you on the road as you came, has sent me that you may receive your sight and be filled with the Holy Spirit." Immediately there fell from his eyes something like scales, and he received his sight at once; and he arose and was baptized. So when he had received food, he was strengthened. Then Saul spent some days with the disciples at Damascus. Immediately he preached the Christ in the synagogues, that He is the Son of God (Acts 9:10-20).

God calls Ananias by name, and his response is, "Here I am, Lord," before he knew his assignment. Sometimes God calls us, and then He tells us what we are to do. Can you imagine hearing the Holy Spirit tell him to find Saul of Tarsus? Ananias could have replied by saying, *"You've got to be kidding? Don't you know he is putting Christians in jail and even killing some?"*

God's love calls Ananias to go beyond his fears, beyond his limited vision, and beyond his understanding to speak a powerful message to Saul about God's redemptive plan and the call of God upon his life. The Lord calls each of us to go beyond what, at the time, makes no sense. He calls us to go beyond our limited vision or understanding and puts something on our lips that changes a person, a group, or a nation for eternity. Obedience opens the way to a great release of His plan; let's look at four ways:

First of all, obedience is releasing our fears, our reluctance and our timidity to the Lord and trusting Him for the outcome. We see where Ananias took the first step as we read, "And Ananias went his way and entered the house" (Acts 9:17a). God wants us to succeed; He does not want us to fail. He takes us beyond a failure mentality and enables us to walk in boldness, confidence, and conviction with a life-changing message.

The act of stepping out demonstrates genuine trust in God, and the result confirms that he heard correctly. This means Ananias has a vital relationship with Jesus Christ to the point that he is familiar with hearing His voice. Jesus teaches, "My sheep hear My voice, and I know them, and they follow Me" (John 10:27). We must be able to hear God—through His Word and in our hearts—before we can obey Him. The Psalmist observes, "The steps of a righteous man are ordered [established] by the Lord, and He delights in his way" (Psalm 37:23). Our fears rob us of co-laboring with the Lord in bringing His Kingdom to be a present reality. God says to each of us, "*Do not fear.*"

Second, obedience is releasing the Word that God has put on our hearts. Back to our story, we read, "Brother Saul, the Lord Jesus, who appeared to you on the road as you came, has sent me that you may receive your sight and be filled with the Holy Spirit" (Acts 9:17b). Who has told

Ananias that Saul had a powerful experience on the Road to Damascus? God did! When Ananias releases his fears, his reluctance, and his timidity, God fills his mouth with precisely what needs to be said. Through His love, God will allow us to see the bigger picture of what He is doing and invite us to co-labor with Him in bringing His purpose to fruition.

The Psalmist states, "My heart was hot within me; while I was musing [mediating], the fire burned. Then I spoke with my tongue" (Psalm 39:3). This speaks of the Holy Spirit burning within us with a message that declares life, health, healing, wholeness, and blessing. Keeping Jesus before us brings good success, and He makes us a blessing. His love takes us beyond our words and thoughts to His Words and His thoughts and sets us ablaze with His message.

Third, obedience is releasing what God has put in you to others: "Immediately there fell from his eyes something like scales, and he received his sight at once; and he arose and was baptized" (Acts 9:18). Ananias went from fear to faith, and from timidity to boldness. He lays his hands on Saul and watches as God removes a covering from his eyes.

Paul describes this transformation in his letter to the Corinthians "But we all, with unveiled face beholding as in a mirror the glory of the Lord, are being transformed into the same image from glory to glory, just as by the Spirit of the Lord" (2 Corinthians 3:18).

Finally, obedience is releasing self to become a new creation; it brings forth change. Saul begins his journey as his own man, and through obedience, he becomes a man of God who now has Good News to share. Luke reports,

"Immediately he preached the Christ in the synagogues, that He is the Son of God" (Acts 9:20).

What if Ananias refuses to go because his fear is greater than his faith? What if he dismisses the thought as not coming from God? We would have missed one of the outstanding fathers of our faith and lost nearly half of the New Testament.

When God asks you to do something, you never know His divine plan for whom you are praying or with whom you are sharing words of encouragement. You may never see the impact of your obedience on this side of heaven, but as Christ's sheep, we are to listen to His voice, and He will successfully lead us to certain people while granting us favor when we encourage and speak blessings. Obedience is walking hand in hand in the love of Jesus as He gives us the grace to do what we can't do in our own strength.

Changed by His Love

Encountering the love of Christ is one of the most transformational experiences one will have. When we grasp how much God loves us, it changes our view of how we see ourselves and how God sees us. Our lives are filled with meaning, purpose, and significance (value and worth). Jesus says, "I am the truth" (John 14:6) which means when we experience the love of Christ, we enter into the truth of what God says about us. The truth sets us free from the things that keep us from really living. The truth frees us and heals our past, assures us as we live in the present, and the power to live the abundant life as Jesus says. Have you encountered the power of the love of Christ? Are we expecting God to show up in unexpected ways that give us a testimony of His goodness and grace? What is the message Christ has assigned you to share with others?

Let all that you do be done in love:

> But the end of all things is at hand; therefore be serious and watchful in your prayers. And above all things have fervent love for one another, for "love will cover a multitude of sins." Be hospitable to one another without grumbling. As each one has received a gift, minister it to one another, as good stewards of the manifold grace of God. If anyone speaks, let him speak as the oracles of God. If anyone ministers, let him do it as with the ability which God supplies, that in all things God may be glorified through Jesus Christ, to whom belong the glory and the dominion forever and ever. Amen (1 Peter 4:7-11).

Agents of Love

We are to be agents of God's love, but why? **First** of all, we love because the divine nature of God lives in us. John writes, "God is love, and he who abides in love abides in God, and God in him" (1 John 4:16). We love because God loved us first as the Bible teaches us: "This is real love—not that we loved God, but that he loved us and sent His Son as a sacrifice to take away our sins...We love each other because He loved us first" (1 John 4:10, 19; NLT). We love because the divine nature of God lives in us, and we can love as He loves because we live in Him, and He lives in us.

Second, we love because it is a sign and indicator of our discipleship of being a follower of Jesus. Scripture says, "A new commandment I give to you, that you love one another; as I have loved you, that you also love one another. By this all will know that you are My disciples, if you have love for one another" (John 13:34-35). What Jesus calls us to do, He will empower us to do. Jesus will help us fulfill His commandment because His commandments are not burdensome (1 John 5:3).

When we belong to Jesus, we are in the household of faith; we are followers of Jesus. This membership identifies who we are and how we are to live out our lives before the Lord, before one another, and before an unbelieving world.

Third, we love because it demonstrates and authenticates that we are a new creation in Jesus Christ. We are to "put on the new man which was created according to God, in true righteousness and holiness" (Ephesians 4:24). The demonstration of God's love through us becomes obvious as we obey the Word which says, "Let us not love in word or in tongue, but in deed and in truth" (1 John 3:18). We know we are a new creation because our fellowship with Jesus Christ leads us to love; we are in a relationship with Him. As a new creation, we think differently, see differently, walk differently, and believe differently. The old way of thinking has passed away, and all things become new.

Fourth, we love because it shows that we are walking in God's light as the Word says, "But if we walk in the light as He is in the light, we have fellowship with one another, and the blood of Jesus Christ His Son cleanses us from all sin" (1 John 1:7). There is either darkness in our hearts or there is light. Light is pure and clear, and it pierces the darkness. Dark and light cannot co-exist.

Fifth, we love from a pure heart as Paul writes, "Since you have purified your souls in obeying the truth through the Spirit in sincere [genuine] love of the brethren, love one another fervently with a pure heart" (1 Peter 1:22). The word "pure" means *without blemish or clean.* Jesus teaches that purity of heart allows us to see God: "Blessed are the pure in heart for they shall see God" (Matthew 5:8). This purity of heart is by grace through faith. Grace describes God's work; faith describes our receiving that work. It is Christ who purifies our hearts so that we can see Him.

Sixth, we love because it covers a multitude of sins. Peter teaches, "Most important of all, continue to show deep love for each other, for love covers a multitude of sins" (1 Peter 4:8, NLT). By loving, we allow God's grace to work in our lives and the lives of others. We have a forgiving spirit as we make allowances for one another's shortcomings.

Seventh, we love because we love God's Word which says that "whoever keeps His word, truly the love of God is perfected in him. By this, we know that we are in Him. He who says he abides in Him ought himself also to walk just as He walked" (1 John 2:5-6). If we do not love His Word, we will not do or practice His Word.

Love is the beginning, the middle, and the end of all things. Through His love, we behold Jesus who makes all things new. Paul tells us that "whatever you do in word or deed, do all in the name of the Lord Jesus, giving thanks to God the Father through Him" (Colossians 3:17). As Christians, we must understand this teaching: "Beloved, if God so loved us, we also ought to love one another" (1 John 4:11). The love of God being poured into our hearts by His Spirit is what takes us beyond a casual acquaintance with the Lord and surface relationships with others, to a vital union with Jesus and sacrificial love for others. His love poured into our hearts by His Spirit takes us beyond our fears, our uncertainty, and our timidity to become powerful witnesses of His transforming power, and we are empowered to love ourselves and to love others. The love of God causes us to transcend—to go beyond—our prejudices, our preconceptions, and our biases. Ananias faces all of these, and God takes him to a place called beyond.

Pivot Points

- We cannot escape the love of God.
- Encountering the love of God is life transformational.
- Following the lead of the Holy Spirit can be challenging.
- God imparts a word that impacts the lives of others.
- God's Word always builds us, equips us, and empowers us to fulfill His plan, purpose, and calling.

Let this be our prayer:

Father, help me to remove the limitations I have put on You or what others have put on You and where I have believed that lie. Please help me to cooperate with You in bringing Your love to touch people, places, and things. I invite You to breathe life, health, and healing into those areas of my life that only Your love can touch and restore. Father, give me a heart to believe that with You nothing is impossible. Amen.

LET'S TALK ABOUT IT

What does it mean to encounter the love of Christ? When have you encountered His love?

Describe Paul's encounter with the love of Christ. How does God's love take him beyond persecuting the church to building up the church?

Ananias had to face his fear to obey God and to pray for Paul. Why is it essential that we face our fears in obeying God?

What does Jesus say is an indicator of our discipleship? How does the love of God change our lives?

Loving others shows that we are walking in the light. What does it mean to walk in God's light?

Which one of the pivot points speaks to you the most? How and in what way?

What is one thing you are going to take away from this lesson?

Lesson 12

GOING BEYOND—WHERE LOVE NEVER FAILS

⌘

The love of God takes us beyond ourselves to demonstrate the love of Christ that brings transformation to the lives of others. God's love is never kept to ourselves, but its purpose is always to be given away. When we have tasted the extravagant love of God, our only response is to pass it on to others. We are looking at several individuals that respond to the love of God, and the different ways that love is expressed. Peter is the one instrument that God uses to bring about a life-changing message with a divine power that results in the transformation of others.

Peter is going throughout the region preaching Jesus and comes to a place called Lydda near Joppa which today would be the southern part of Tel Aviv. We want to look at two individuals who encounter the love of God through Peter and whose lives are transformed by that love. The first individual is Aeneas who has been paralyzed for eight years but is gripped with the message and power which Peter preaches.

There are several things about these accounts that are worth noting. **First** of all, the church is experiencing the wonderful love and power of Christ and enjoying the presence of the Holy Spirit: "So the church throughout all

Judea and Galilee and Samaria had peace and was being built up" (Acts 9:31a, ESV). **Second,** there was a great reverence of the Lord because of the mighty signs, wonders, and miracles that are taking place—a sense of awe prevails (Acts 9:31b). **Third,** the church was experiencing the presence of the Holy Spirit as He is very much among them; they were "walking...in the comfort of the Holy Spirit" (Acts 9:31c, ESV).

There is a sense of anticipation among the believers that God is doing something different. This is all new for them because they have never seen anything like this.

This chapter will show how the early church does not consider the cost of what sharing the gospel might mean to them; they are driven by love. They see their mission field as the least, the last, and the lost, and their goal is to touch people with the life-transforming power of Jesus Christ. We will learn that simple obedience opens the door for the gospel and that it is important to make ourselves available to God to use however He desires.

Aeneas Responds to the Love of Christ

Luke, the writer of Acts and also a doctor, likes to provide details of the physical problems people were having so that we can get the message of God's great love that knows no boundaries of what He can do.

> Then the churches throughout all Judea, Galilee, and Samaria had peace and were edified. And walking in the fear of the Lord and in the comfort of the Holy Spirit, they were multiplied. Now it came to pass, as

> Peter went through all parts of the country, that he also came down to the saints who dwelt in Lydda. There he found a certain man named Aeneas, who had been bedridden eight years and was paralyzed. And Peter said to him, "Aeneas, Jesus the Christ heals you. Arise and make your bed." Then he arose immediately. So all who dwelt at Lydda and Sharon saw him and turned to the Lord (Acts 9:31-35).

While Peter is preaching Jesus to the people and all are giving him their attention, but there is one man who gets **his** attention. We don't know why Peter is drawn to this man or what he is doing that catches Peter's eye, but of all the people present the Holy Spirit tells Peter to speak these words of life to Aeneas. Let's go over some thoughts that we can glean from these verses:

The **first** thing I notice is that Peter knows the man's name. Does the Holy Spirit give Peter a word of knowledge that his name is Aeneas? If so, that makes the miracle even more significant. Have they been in conversation earlier and God puts it on Peter's heart to declare the Lord's healing over his life? Regardless, this is a notable miracle, and we cannot dismiss it. Peter wants the people to know that Jesus is the way, the truth, and the life and that Jesus, through the Holy Spirit, is present to heal.

The **second** thing that catches my attention is that Peter does not pray for Aeneas. He simply declares that Jesus is his healer: "Aeneas, Jesus Christ heals you" (Acts 9:34). Peter is saying, "*I do not have the ability to heal you, but I know the One who can heal you, and His name is Jesus.*"

The **third** thing of note is that Peter gives him direction about what he needs to do in response to his healing: "Arise and make your bed" (Acts 9:34). Aeneas' only response is to get up as Peter describes: "Then he arose immediately" (v. 34). What else could Aeneas do? What could he do when his name is mentioned before a crowd of people and everyone is watching? What do you think he is going to do? Get up!

The **fourth** thing is that this miracle becomes the platform for a yet greater work. We see this greater work when the entire community comes to confess Christ as Lord in response to seeing this miracle. Luke records the event: "So all who dwelt at Lydda and Sharon saw him and turned to the Lord" (Acts 9:35). The thing that gets people's attention is that they know Aeneas and see his healing with their own eyes; his miracle is indisputable proof of God's amazing love.

As Peter speaks these healing words, he opens a door for multitudes to come and know Jesus and His life-giving Spirit. When something wonderful happens through the Holy Spirit, there is always a ripple effect that has a profound impact on the kingdom of God.

This story emphasizes to us that as we open our hearts to the Lord and respond to what He says, our miracle—our breakthrough—is just around the corner. It may happen unexpectedly, but the Lord knows all about us, even before we share our needs. He knows that our greatest need is to encounter His love and respond to that love with an open and receptive heart to what God wants to do in our lives that demonstrate His glory, grace, and goodness.

Tabitha Responds to the Love of Christ

Responding to the love of Christ is one of the most life-changing experiences one will ever have. In our search for those who encounter the love of Christ in the book of Acts, we find an influential person named Tabitha who becomes sick and dies. The community hears that Peter is in the area and invite him to come down to pray for her. Dr. C. Peter Wagner describes Tabitha whose Aramaic name is Dorcas as:

> One of the highly respected women of the church... She was respected because of her many good deeds done through her obvious spiritual gifts of mercy and service. Undoubtedly she was an affluent woman.
>
> —C. Peter Wagner
>
> ***The Book of Acts: A Commentary***[9]

> At Joppa there was a certain disciple named Tabitha, which is translated Dorcas. This woman was full of good works and charitable deeds which she did. But it happened in those days that she became sick and died. When they had washed her, they laid her in an upper room. And since Lydda was near Joppa, and the disciples had heard that Peter was there, they sent two men to him, imploring him not to delay in coming to them. Then Peter arose and went with them. When he had come, they brought him to the upper room. And all the widows stood by him weeping, showing the tunics and garments which Dorcas had made while she was with them. But Peter put them all out, and knelt down and prayed. And turning to the body he said, "Tabitha, arise." And she opened her eyes, and when she saw Peter she sat up.

> Then he gave her his hand and lifted her up; and when he had called the saints and widows, he presented her alive. And it became known throughout all Joppa, and many believed on the Lord. So it was that he stayed many days in Joppa with Simon, a tanner (Acts 9:36-43).

We do not know if the disciples have encountered raising the dead before this, but when Jesus sends out the disciples according to Matthew 10:8, He tells them to "heal the sick, cleanse the lepers, raise the dead, cast out demons." Luke, a recognized doctor, reports that Tabitha is deceased. What we find among the believers in Joppa is a high level of faith to ask Peter to walk three hours from Lydda to Joppa to pray for Tabitha.

The Bible makes it clear that when he arrives in her room, Peter "knelt down and prayed" (Acts 9:40). Don't you wonder what he prays? Could it be he was making sure it was God's will for her to be raised from the dead? After he kneels and prays, he senses a release in his spirit to pray for her life to be restored. I wonder if Peter's prayer went something like this, "*Father, I bring this dear saint of God before You and ask that You honor the prayers of the church and restore life to her.*" At this point, Tabitha sits up, and the church rejoices to see her alive.

This is the first case mentioned in Acts of raising the dead. What do we learn from this powerful encounter of responding to the love of God that restores one person to life and transforms an entire community? Yes, there have been hundreds of accounts throughout the world where believers have been raised from the dead, and more and more books are being written on this subject. In the

Western world, it is hard for us to get our hearts and minds around such a thing as raising the dead; however, God's great love continues to bring forth miracles today.

Let's examine four principles in responding to the love of God. The **first** principle is don't limit God (Acts 9:38). This Christian community in Joppa believes that God will do something miraculous for Tabitha. They are unaware that religion dictates that you cannot ask God to raise someone from the dead; no one told them this could not be done.

Most of the limitations we put on God are what others have told us that He can't do or doesn't do anymore.

What would happen if we took off the limitations we put on God because of what others have said? People often put limitations on God because of their own experiences, not considering what God's Word says about life, finances, health, healing, and miracles. The problem with this is we have believed the lies. Let's not limit the Creator of the Universe!

The **second** principle in responding to God's love is cooperating with Him (Acts 9:39a). Peter is an eyewitness of profound healings and miracles as he is led to pray or speak words of healing. God calls us to do things that stretch our faith and cause us to cooperate with Him. As Peter ministers to others, God pours out His love through him in a way that requires his faith and cooperation to manifest God's will and ultimately impacts the Christian community in a universal way.

One example of a personal encounter I have had with God's love was while I was taking my daily walk when I was pastoring. I found myself struggling about a church situation which demanded that I intervene with a plan of action. In the middle of a public park and from out of nowhere, two complete strangers step out in faith and cooperate with God as they come up to me and ask, "Is there anything we can pray with you about?" I immediately responded, "Yes, there is!" and told them of my prayer need. We joined hands right there in the middle of the park and prayed. Their obedience and cooperation with God's plan brought me great relief and faith that God is an ever-present help to direct me in my time of need!

The **third** principle of responding to God's love is to find others who will agree with you in prayer. Sometimes you have to close the door on doubt and unbelief as we see in this story: "And all the widows stood by him weeping, showing the tunics and garments which Dorcas had made while she was with them. But Peter put them all out" (Acts 9:39b-40a). Peter's response is to do what he sees Jesus do in His ministry (Luke 7:13-14; Matthew 9:23-26). Peter puts aside doubt, fear, and unbelief because he knows that agreeing in prayer moves mountains.

If you need a breakthrough, find someone who will stand and agree with you for that breakthrough. Jesus says, "If two of you agree on earth concerning anything that they ask it, will be done for them by My Father in heaven" (Matthew 18:19).

The **fourth** principle in responding to the love of Christ is to declare life where there seems to be no life. We see this in Peter's life when he "knelt down and prayed. And turning to the body he **said, 'Tabitha, arise'**" (Acts 9:40, emphasis added). In the Old Testament, we see the prophet Ezekiel speaks life over that which was dead, and God raises the dead (Ezekiel 37:1-10).

What are we declaring over our lives, our community, our families, and our church? We should be speaking life to dead bones that God will raise up a mighty army to follow Him. Tabitha responds to the life-giving words of Peter: "And she opened her eyes, and when she saw Peter she sat up. Then he gave her his hand and lifted her up; and when he had called the saints and widows, he presented her alive" (Acts 9:40b-41). Those who were weeping are now celebrating. The response of the believers to this miracle is to lift the limitations of what God can do; they are now able to cooperate with God's purpose and agree together that God can raise the dead: "And it became known throughout all Joppa, and many believed on the Lord" (Acts 9:42).

God's grace working in our lives reminds us that everything is not about us, but about Him and the powerful transformation He has made and continues to make in us. Jesus asks persons of every walk of life to follow Him. We all have a past, but it does not stop us from being used by God, nor does it define us. We are all a work in progress, and God's extravagant love draws us to Himself so that we reflect His image in all that we do. The truth is we can hold the Lord at bay and never experience the depth of His mercy and grace and the outpouring of His extravagant love and affection. When we keep the Lord at bay, we miss His best for us. God promises that when we draw near to Him, He will draw near to us (James 4:8). We want His presence—His nearness—as He leads us in the way we should go. When we draw close to the Lord, we experience the depth of His love for us.

May you experience, right now, the extravagant love of Jesus, His liberating power, and His grace that is more than enough to complete you, to heal you, and to satisfy the deepest longings of your heart.

We can be in church and lost: lost our way, lost our vision, lost our purpose, lost our first love for Jesus, lost our passion for Him, and lost our desire for purity and holiness. As our elder brother, Christ comes to seek us out and bring us home with Him. He comes to us in our feeling of being lost and imparts hope, promise, and joy. The Bible states, "'You will seek me and find me, when you seek me with all your heart. I will be found by you, declares the Lord'" (Jeremiah 29:13-14a, ESV).

An Eye-Opening Experience Unveils the Power of Christ

> Now as Jesus passed by, He saw a man who was blind from birth. And His disciples asked Him, saying, "Rabbi, who sinned, this man or his parents, that he was born blind?" Jesus answered, "Neither this man nor his parents sinned, but that the works of God should be revealed in him. I must work the works of Him who sent Me while it is day; the night is coming when no one can work. As long as I am in the world, I am the light of the world." When He had said these things, He spat on the ground and made clay with the saliva; and He anointed the eyes of the blind man with the clay. And He said to him, "Go, wash in the

> pool of Siloam" (which is translated, Sent). So he went and washed, and came back seeing. Therefore the neighbors and those who previously had seen that he was blind said, "Is not this he who sat and begged?" Some said, "This is he." Others said, "He is like him." He said, "I am he." Therefore they said to him, "How were your eyes opened?" He answered and said, "A Man called Jesus made clay and anointed my eyes and said to me, 'Go to the pool of Siloam and wash.' So I went and washed, and I received sight." Then they said to him, "Where is He? He said, "I do not know" (John 9:1-12).

Let's examine this passage of Scripture to observe God's power. **First** of all, the mighty works of God are revealed.

Jesus says, "I must work the works of Him who sent Me while it is day; the night is coming when no one can work" (John 9:4). There is that sense of divine urgency—a sense of mission and purpose—that Jesus came to complete. Every miracle or sign points to something that Jesus wants us to learn. Signs are not an end in themselves, but a means of pointing us to Jesus. In this incident, we find that this sign is telling us: "The works of God should be revealed in [the man]" (John 9:3). The word "reveal" means *to uncover, to make visible, to make known what had not been known before, and to make clear.* God's power is made known by His works. Jesus is saying I am revealing the will of God for humanity; I am revealing what believers will do in My name.

Jesus says, *"I am revealing the ministry that those who believe in Me will continue when I go back to My Father."* It is not just a story about a man receiving his sight, but a story where the divine purposes of God are revealed. This is the reason for the divine urgency of Jesus in revealing the mission and purpose for which He came. His purpose is to equip believers with the faith to continue the works He reveals through His signs.

Second, the ministry of Jesus is unconventional.

John reports,"[Jesus] spat on the ground and made clay with the saliva; and He anointed the eyes of the blind man with clay" (John 9:6). Jesus is not confined nor obligated to do the same thing all the time in the same way. This behavior is commonly called a rut—it is a coffin with both ends knocked out. Jesus refuses to be put into a mold when He uses whatever is available to Him to release a miracle—to reveal that He who is in the midst of them is mighty. Jesus operates outside the box then and now.

Third, the command of Jesus requires faith.

Jesus said to this young man to "'go, wash in the pool of Siloam'...So he went and washed, and came back seeing" (John 9:7). We choose to respond to the word Jesus has given us to see that it comes to fruition. This man responds in faith to the revelation that Jesus gives Him, and he comes back seeing. With every act of obedience, comes a witness to the mighty acts of God. The man's neighbors ask him how he is healed, and he answers, "A Man called Jesus made clay and anointed my eyes and said to me, 'Go to the pool of Siloam and wash.' So I went and washed, and I received sight" (John 9:11). The word Siloam means *sent*. Jesus sends him out with a purpose.

Fourth, God's power fills us with boldness.

When questioned by the religious leaders, the healed man says, "I told you already, and you did not listen. Why do you want to hear it again? Do you also want to become His disciples?" (John 9:27). What does this say about the transformation Jesus makes? The man becomes mighty in speech, and he boldly replies, "'Why, this is a marvelous thing, that you do not know where He is from; yet He has opened my eyes!'" (John 9:30). In effect, he was asking, "*And you are supposed to be our spiritual leaders?*" This man stands in the strength that God gives him. The man went on to say, "'Since the world began it has been unheard of that anyone opened the eyes of one who was born blind'" (John 9:32). The man is saying, "*God is doing a new thing.*"

There is a price to be paid for walking in the truth of God's revealed purpose and plan. The religious community is angered at what he is saying: "'You were completely born in sins, and are you teaching us?' And they cast him out" (John 9:34). This man walks in the revealed purpose of God for his life and pays a price for it.

Fifth, miracles make believers out of you.

This powerful encounter leads the man to place his trust and belief in Jesus to begin a transformed life.

> Jesus heard that they had cast him out; and when He had found him, He said to him. "Do you believe in the Son of God?" The man responded, "Who is He, Lord, that I may believe in Him?" Jesus said, "You have both seen [revelation] Him and it is He who is

> talking with you." The man replied, "Lord, I believe!" and he worshiped Him" (John 9:35-38).

When we encounter Jesus, it brings us to a place of trust, belief, and worship. This is why miracles make believers out of us.

Pivot Points

- People respond to words of healing and wholeness.
- Speaking words of life infuse hope and a new beginning.
- God meets us where we are and lifts us out of circumstances.
- God takes us beyond our hopelessness and fills us with abundant life.
- Miracles make believers out of you.

Let our prayer be:

Father, help me to receive all that You have for me so that I might see and experience Your profound love for me. Open my eyes to see the display of Your glory and wonder so that I may speak boldly of Your transforming power. Father, help me to pick up the assignment You have for me and to behold the beauty of Your grace, love, and power. Father, give me a heart to believe that with You nothing is impossible. Amen.

LET'S TALK ABOUT IT

What does it mean that God's love never fails?

How did Aeneas respond to the love of God?

How can the Good News of Christ open doors for people to respond to Christ?

How did Tabitha respond to the love of God, and how did this impact the community?

There were four principles to responding to the love of God. Which one of these four spoke to you the most and why?

What can take us beyond the limitations we put on God to believe that with Him nothing is impossible?

Which one of the pivot points speaks to you the most? How and in what way?

What is one thing you are going to take away from this lesson?

Lesson 13

GOING BEYOND—A FAITH WORTH SHARING

⌘

As we continue in the book of Acts, let's look at what happens when people encounter the love of Jesus, what results from that encounter, and the transformation that takes place. ***Merriam-Webster Dictionary*** defines "encounter" as m*eeting unexpectedly; a meeting with a person or thing, especially a casual, unexpected, or brief meeting*. More often than not, a divine appointment with God's love has unexpected results. We find this illustrated in Acts 3 when Peter and John go to worship and pray at the temple and find a man who is paralyzed, sitting outside the temple at the gate called Beautiful begging for money. The man's plight gives Peter and John the opportunity to go beyond and step into God's call. At the Beautiful Gate, the lame man has a divine appointment with God's love introduced by those with "beautiful feet...who preach the gospel of peace, who bring glad tidings of good things" (Romans 10:15) which brings him unexpected healing. Christ's love inspires the early church to welcome the least, the last, and the lost and do whatever is necessary to bring people to an encounter with the living God.

This chapter is about seeing ourselves, others, and God's call upon our lives from God's viewpoint. His love has been poured into our hearts by the Holy Spirit (Romans 5:5); that's what gives us a faith

worth sharing. Like the disciples, our lives should be fueled by the love of God and by a desire to see others experience the living Christ.

Changed Before Our Very Eyes

> Now Peter and John went up together to the temple at the hour of prayer, the ninth hour. And a certain man lame from his mother's womb was carried, whom they laid daily at the gate of the temple which is called Beautiful, to ask alms from those who entered the temple; who, seeing Peter and John about to go into the temple, asked for alms. And fixing his eyes on him, with John, Peter said, "Look at us." So he gave them his attention, expecting to receive something from them. Then Peter said, "Silver and gold I do not have, but what I do have I give you: In the name of Jesus Christ of Nazareth, rise up and walk." And he took him by the right hand and lifted him up, and immediately his feet and anklebones received strength. So he, leaping up, stood and walked and entered the temple with them—walking, leaping, and praising God. And all the people saw him walking and praising God. Then they knew that it was he who sat begging alms at the Beautiful Gate of the temple; and they were filled with wonder and amazement at what had happened to him (Acts 3:1-10).

First of all, the lame man is offered something he is not expecting to receive: "Peter said, 'Look at us.' So he [gives] them his attention, expecting to receive something from them. Then Peter said, 'Silver and gold I do not have, but what I do have I give you: In the name of Jesus Christ of

Nazareth, rise up and walk'" (Acts 3:4-6). Peter first establishes eye contact before he speaks words to change the man's life from this point on. Peter gives him something worth far more than silver and gold: an invitation to encounter the love of God. The gift being offered was free, and it only needed to be received and acted upon by faith. This encounter causes the man to experience something he is not expecting. He is not expecting words of kindness, compassion, and good news. This truly gets his attention.

Second, the words Peter speaks releases not just hope, but also a new way of living: "Rise and walk." Again, we see the disciples doing no more or no less than what they see Jesus do. He is their model, and they are simply doing what they see modeled. God uses people just like you and me to touch the lives of others because the same Holy Spirit that lived in them lives in us.

Third, encountering the love of Jesus makes an immediate difference in the lame man's life: "And Peter took him by the right hand and lifted him up, and immediately his feet and ankle bones received strength" (Acts 3:7). The touch of Christ upon a life causes something to happen immediately. Again, Peter sees Jesus take those He healed by the hand, and Peter did likewise as He watches God put a new step in this man's life, "So he, leaping up, stood and walked and entered the temple with them—walking, leaping, and praising God" (v. 8).

Last, encountering the love of Jesus impacts those around us: "And all the people saw him walking and praising God...and they were filled with wonder and amazement at what had happened to him" (Acts 3:9-10). This is the good news Peter is giving to this man, and it touches him physically, mentally, emotionally, and spiritually. He could now feel differently, think differently, and believe differently.

Our Walk of Faith

When we encounter the love of God, we are able to pass on our faith to others. As we keep focused on Jesus and His work, we find that the Lord helps us in our walk.

First of all, God gives us the strength and **power** to get up and walk. He "strengthen[s] the hands which hang down, and the feeble knees" (Hebrews 12:12). Peter touches the lame man at the Beautiful Gate, and he "[takes] him by the right hand and lift[s] him up, and immediately his feet and anklebones receive strength" (Acts 3:7). We also see that when Aeneas is touched by the power of God, he gets up immediately (Acts 9:32-35). The fact that we can get up again when we have been knocked down causes others to look to Jesus.

Second, God gives us a new step in our walk. The writer of Hebrews says that God "make[s] straight paths for your feet" (Hebrews 12:13a). The lame man at the Gate Beautiful has a spring in his step that was not there before his healing: "So he, leaping up, stood and walked and entered the temple with them—walking, leaping, and praising God" (Acts 3:8). People see evidence of your new step, and they look to Jesus as they do with the lame man from Lystra who leaps when he is touched by God (Acts 14:8-11).

Third, God gives us the ability to walk forward—to keep moving. Our past is behind; the only way ahead is to go forward. Each step we take is a testimony to others of God's grace and love. Paul exhorts us to press forward not backward, when he says, "But one thing I do, forgetting those things which are behind and reaching forward to those things that are ahead" (Philippians 3:13).

As we keep our eyes focused on Jesus, God gives us the power to get up and walk. The evidence of His presence in our lives puts a new step in our walk so we can start moving forward beyond what we thought or imagined.

From time to time, we all need a hand on our journey. When strength is fleeting, we can count on the hand of Christ reaching out to us as Isaiah prophecies: "Fear not, for I am with you; be not dismayed, for I am your God. I will strengthen you, Yes, I will help you, I will uphold you with My righteous right hand (Isaiah 41:10).

- The hand of Christ reaches down to give us the lift we need out of what holds us down.
- The hand of Christ stretches out to touch us at our point of weakness and strengthens us.
- The hand of Christ is extended to take us out of our failures, shortcomings, disappointment, and the wounds we have encountered in life and to give us His peace.
- The hand of Christ reaches deep into our hearts and does a powerful and transforming work we could never have apart from Him.

The encounter with the disciples sharing the good news to the lame man at the Beautiful Gate is an extension of the hand of Christ that causes us to rise and walk out of what has held us captive. We rise and walk out of the oppression and depression that constantly plagues us. We rise and walk out of the poor image we have of ourselves. We rise and walk out of the words that wound us. We rise and walk out of the sense of disappointment and heartache we have experienced. We rise and walk out of our fears into His freedom. We rise and walk out from under the load we carry that we were never intended to carry.

Miracles Open Doors

> Now as the lame man who was healed held on to Peter and John, all the people ran together to them in the porch which is called Solomon's, greatly amazed. So when Peter saw it, he responded to the people: "Men of Israel, why do you marvel at this? Or why look so intently at us, as though by our own power or godliness we had made this man walk? The God of Abraham, Isaac, and Jacob, the God of our fathers, glorified His Servant Jesus, whom you delivered up and denied in the presence of Pilate, when he was determined to let Him go. But you denied the Holy One and the Just, and asked for a murderer to be granted to you, and killed the Prince of life, whom God raised from the dead, of which we are witnesses. And His name, through faith in His name, has made this man strong, whom you see and know. Yes, the faith which comes through Him has given him this perfect soundness in the presence of you all" (Acts 3:11-16).

This miracle provides a platform from which Peter preaches about Jesus saying, "There is no other name under heaven given among men by which we must be saved" (Acts 4:12). The fruit of this encounter causes the kingdom of God to grow by 5,000 people coming to Christ (Acts 4:4). It creates a place where the disciples receive a powerful infilling of the Holy Spirit and speak the word with boldness (Acts 4:31). Encountering the love of Christ is life-changing in a personal way, and then it impacts everyone around us bringing others to experience the love of Christ for themselves.

In what way do we need to encounter the unconditional love of Christ? What would it mean to hear the words of Christ: "Rise and walk?" In what way do we need to experience the hand of Christ reaching down and giving us the lift that only He can give? May we be a people through whom the love of Christ reaches the last, the least, and the lost.

Impact of the Resurrected Life

Peter shares what the people had done to Jesus as they crucify the Lord of glory:

> "But you denied the Holy One and the Just [blameless, righteous], and asked for a murderer to be granted to you, and killed the Prince [Originator] of life, whom God raised from the dead, of which we are witnesses" (Acts 3:14-15).

The message of the resurrection carries the power of personal testimony: "And with great power the apostles gave witness to the resurrection of the Lord Jesus. And great grace was upon them all" (Acts 4:33). God calls us to Himself, puts His Spirit within us, and sends us out to do the things He did while on the earth (Matthew 10:1).

Evidence of living the resurrected life:

- **A changed life**
  "Now we believe, not because of what you said, for we ourselves have heard Him and we know that this is indeed the Christ, the Savior of the world" (John 4:42).
- **A forgiven life**
  "In Him we have redemption [the purchase paid for our freedom] through His blood, the forgiveness of sins, according to the riches of His grace" (Ephesians 1:7). "To Him all the prophets witness that, through His name, whoever believes in Him will receive remission [forgiveness] of sins" (Acts 10:43).
- **An overcoming life**
  "Who is he who overcomes the world, but he who believes that Jesus is the Son of God" (1 John 5:5).
- **A blessed life**
  "Blessed is the man who trusts in the Lord" (Jeremiah 17:7).

The message of the resurrection creates transformation: "However, many of those who heard the word believed; and the number of the men came to be about five thousand" (Acts 4:4). We are the aroma of Christ to others, the fragrance of the life of Christ in us (Ephesians 5:2).

The message of the resurrection creates an atmosphere that is filled with holy expectancy, an atmosphere that is filled with great faith, an atmosphere that is filled with heavenly praise, and an atmosphere that is filled with dynamic response.

The message of the resurrection sets the captive free: "And His name, through faith in His name, has made this man strong, whom you see and know. Yes, the faith which comes through Him has given him this perfect soundness in the presence of you all" (Acts 3:16).

The disciples are given a **transforming** message which is: "Go into all the world and preach the gospel to every creature" (Mark 16:15). God's work through the disciples includes:

- They will cast out demons (Mark 16:17).
- They will be given Spirit-inspired languages (Mark 16:17).
- They will have God's protective hand upon them (Mark 16:18).
- They will see signs of healing and wholeness (Mark 16:18).
- They will give the promise of His presence working with them (Mark 16:20).

Going Where We Are Sent

Throughout history when the body of Christ has suffered persecutions, hardships, and trials of all sorts, the church has flourished. It has grown stronger, not weaker. It has increased, not decreased. The witness of the church does not become powerless, but rather powerful. The first-century church is being assaulted on all sides and is forced to spread out of Jerusalem and the uttermost parts of the world. God uses this time when the church experiences great pressure from the world to send out His people everywhere to turn the world upside down. It creates a powerful movement that will only end when Jesus returns for His church.

This time in church history is known as the great Dispersion when Christians spread throughout the known world carrying the Good News of the gospel of Jesus Christ as Mark in his Gospel explains, "And they went out and preached everywhere, the Lord working with them and confirming the Word through the accompanying signs" (Mark 16:20).

Let's look briefly at one man's experience of learning to share his faith. Philip is not one of the twelve disciples; he is simply a believer in Jesus Christ who has a transforming experience. It is possible that he may have been one of the 3,000 that come to Christ on the day of Pentecost. His experience makes him willing to step out in obedience and go where God commands him.

> Now an angel of the Lord spoke to Philip, saying, "Arise and go toward the south along the road which goes down from Jerusalem to Gaza." This is desert. So he arose and went. And behold, a man of Ethiopia, a eunuch of great authority under Candace the queen of the Ethiopians, who had charge of all her treasury, and had come to Jerusalem to worship, was returning. And sitting in his chariot, he was reading Isaiah the prophet. Then the Spirit said to

> Philip, "Go near and overtake this chariot." So Philip ran to him, and heard him reading the prophet Isaiah, and said, "Do you understand what you are reading?" And he said, "How can I, unless someone guides me?" And he asked Philip to come up and sit with him. The place in the Scripture which he read was this: "He was led as a sheep to the slaughter; And as a lamb before its shearer is silent, So He opened not His mouth. In His humiliation His justice was taken away, And who will declare His generation? For His life is taken from the earth." So the eunuch answered Philip and said, "I ask you, of whom does the prophet say this, of himself or of some other man?" Then Philip opened his mouth, and beginning at this Scripture, preached Jesus to him. Now as they went down the road, they came to some water. And the eunuch said, "See, here is water. What hinders me from being baptized?" Then Philip said, "If you believe with all your heart, you may." And he answered and said, "I believe that Jesus Christ is the Son of God." So he commanded the chariot to stand still. And both Philip and the eunuch went down into the water, and he baptized him. Now when they came up out of the water, the Spirit of the Lord caught Philip away, so that the eunuch saw him no more; and he went on his way rejoicing (Acts 8:26-39).

What does "obedience" mean? What does it look like? **First** of all, obedience means cooperating with God's plan; a simple "yes" is all that is needed. An explanation is not necessary because God is absolutely trustworthy and His ability to lead us is greater than the enemies' ability to deceive us. Philip's response to God is described: "So he arose and went…" (Acts 8:27). The first principle Philip is learning about sharing his faith is that obedience is required. Let's call it making ourselves available to God.

Philip first and foremost is a bearer of the Good News of Jesus, because it has become Good News to him personally. Jesus fills Philip's heart, and the life of Jesus is simply spilling over in all that he does. Philip's sharing/witnessing came out of a personal relationship with Jesus. The instructions given are just enough to get him moving. Philip's response is to get up and go.

Philip does not ask why; he just obeys. He leaves a revival to go to Gaza—a place that may not have been familiar to him. Again, the Lord does not mind if we ask questions; we just don't want to talk ourselves out of going when He says, "*I am sending you.*" God gives Philip enough information to start with and more would be given when he gets there. God simply asks us to cooperate with Him.

> God responds to people who cooperate with His promises and with the nature of His kingdom. He exposes us to possibilities, summons us through opportunities, and invites us to co-labor with Him to see His Kingdom manifest among humanity.
>
> —Bill Johnson, ***Defining Moments*** [10]

Second, obedience means waiting for further instruction. "Then the Spirit said to Philip, 'Go near and overtake this chariot'" (Acts 8:29). Philip is beginning to realize what is taking place, but he does not rush into the situation; he waits for the Lord to show him his next step. This is a real key: don't get ahead of the Lord, nor lag behind what He is doing, but stay in step with Him with anticipation. Philip is learning to trust the Holy Spirit, the Helper—the One called alongside us. It is the Holy Spirit who creates a hunger and thirst for more. As one person has said, "God creates a vacuum in the hearts of men and women that only He can fill."

Third, obedience means listening to what the Spirit is saying. For Philip, the Spirit is leading him to ask the eunuch a simple question "'Do you understand what you are reading'" (Acts 8:30)? He listens to the Spirit's leading to open a door of conversation. The eunuch replies, "'How can I, unless someone guides me?' And he asked Philip to come up and sit with him" (Acts 8:31). All this happens as a result of simple obedience. The Holy Spirit is at work preparing the hearts of people while he directs our witness.

In obedience, Philip "open[s] his mouth and beginning at this Scripture, preached Jesus to him" (Acts 8:35). Philip may not have known what to say, but we find a promise that says, "Open your mouth wide, and I will fill it" (Psalm 81:10). Faith sharing is not about us, but about Jesus and the overwhelming love He has for people. Philip, "preached Jesus to him," not his experience, not a list of dos and don'ts, not "*if you are good enough*," not "*if you attend synagogue/church*," but Philip shares Jesus with the eunuch. Philip is learning to present the Good News of Jesus Christ in a winsome way. The Ethiopian response to this was, "I believe that Jesus Christ is the Son of God" (Acts 8:37).

I believe one of the reasons Philip is able to present the Good News of Jesus clearly is found in Acts 2:42 where it tells us, "And they continued steadfastly in the apostles' doctrine and fellowship, in the breaking of bread, and in prayers." The key to equipping believers to present the gospel with simplicity, confidence, and the empowerment of the Holy Spirit is study, fellowship, and prayer.

Fourth, obedience means openness to what God is doing at that moment. The eunuch saw the water and asks, "'What hinders me from being baptized?' Then Philip said, 'If you believe with all your heart, you may.' And he answered and said, 'I believe that Jesus Christ is the Son of God'" (Acts 8:36b-37). In that moment, Philip is open to what God is doing in the eunuch. Remember where we started? It all begins with simple obedience that leads Philip to this man who is hungry to know more and respond to the gospel. Then the eunuch took this message to his own people and to his own country.

This Ethiopian takes the powerful message of Jesus to Africa where it spreads throughout the continent. Obedience will fill our life with good fruit. Jesus says that we "'should go and bear fruit, and that your fruit should remain'" (John 15:16). The truth is that He who begins a good work in us will bring it to maturity. As the Lord takes us from faith to faith, from grace to grace, and from glory to glory, we bear witness to the transforming work Christ has made, is making, and will continue to make in our lives. For Philip, it means to enjoy the ride to yet another adventure the Lord has for him: "Now when they came up out of the water, the Spirit of the Lord caught Philip away, so that the eunuch saw him no more; and he went on his way rejoicing" (Acts 8:39). The life of obedience is full of adventure.

Obedience to the Great Commission

Jesus' command to His disciples in the Great Commission is to "go therefore and make disciples" (Matthew 28:19). There is a sense of urgency that we are to be busy making disciples; this is not optional for those who decide to follow Jesus. Disciples are made when we "go into all the world and preach the gospel" (Mark 16:15). It is plain to see that the gospel must be preached in order to produce disciples. Jesus continues to tell the disciples what to teach: "And that repentance and remission of sins should be preached in His name to all nations" (Luke 24:47). This is an urgent message that Jesus gives to His disciples so they will share their faith with others as the Spirit leads them.

> Evangelism is not a priority to most Christians. Less than one out of ten said that they have ever intentionally built a relationship with someone in the hope of being able to lead that person to Christ.
>
> —George Barna, ***Growing True Disciples*** [11]

The first thing in fulfilling the Great Commission is to be a witness. In order to be an effective witness, these three statements may help you develop your testimony:

- What was my life like before I came to Christ?
- How did I become aware that I needed Christ?
- What has my life been like since I received Christ?

Faith sharing may not be in the form of the "Four-Spiritual Laws" or some method or technique we learn. It may be in just going through life as a living epistle (2 Corinthians 3:3)—keeping our relationship with Jesus up to date.

Key elements to faith sharing: The elements to faith sharing are obedience and making ourselves available to the Lord. We trust the Holy Spirit to prepare the hearts of others and to fill our mouths with the good things of God. We seek to be equipped to confidently share Christ, His love, His forgiveness, and the transformation that only He can make.

How do we share our faith?

With meekness and reverence. The Bible says, "Always be ready to give a defense to everyone who asks you a reason for the hope that is in you, with meekness" (1 Peter 3:15).

With confidence and boldness. The early Christians "were all filled with the Holy Spirit, and they spoke the word of God with boldness" (Acts 4:31b).

With humility and gratitude. We are to "be clothed with humility" (1 Peter 5:5). As we are humble, we will find God's grace manifested in our lives. Scripture says, "God gives grace to the humble" (James 4:6b).

Living a focused life involves connecting people to Jesus by being obedient to the Great Commission.

Pivot Points

- Our lives change when we look to Jesus.
- Sharing our faith gives someone the lift they need.
- Miracles open the door for a life-transforming message.
- Being open to the prompts of the Holy Spirit leads to effective ministry.

- When we open our mouths to speak on God's behalf, He always fills it with good things.

Let this be our prayer:

Father, strengthen me in my inner man to be bold and courageous in sharing my faith with others. Father, help me to obey you promptly and with a joyful heart. Father, thank You for the leadership of the Holy Spirit that always leads me to the right places and to the right people. Father, let me encounter Your mighty presence and the extravagance of Your love. May I be a communicator and demonstrator of Your love to the world and live transformed. Father, give me holy boldness to see Your Kingdom come and Your will done on earth as it is in heaven. Amen!

A Final Word

I trust this journey of going beyond and stepping into the greatness of God's love and His empowering grace has touched your life in a refreshing way that fills you with hope and promise. Through our study, we have found that God takes us beyond our greatest fears, our sense of defeat and loss, and through the times of spiritual drought and brings us to a place of overcoming. We discover that God never leaves us and whatever comes against us we can rest assured that God will make a way where there seems to be no way and enables us to stand up under it and be victorious.

We have seen through the lives of biblical characters that when they are tested, they pass the test because they know that God is with them and gives them words of assurance and promise of what He is going to do. It is through the accounts and witness of these men and women that we, too, can rest assured that when God comes to their aid, He will also come to our aid. Remember, Jesus is the same yesterday, today, and forever. What He has done for others, He will do for us.

Finally, I hope that you have been encouraged in your faith to believe that your case is not too difficult for God. That through this book, God has deposited in you a hope that will never fade away, but a hope that rests in the eternal promises of God that He is greater than any problem, obstacle, or setback you will ever encounter. May the love of God, the peace of Christ, and the power of the Holy Spirit be upon you.

LET'S TALK ABOUT IT

Why is the lame man not expecting what he receives from Peter and John?

What are the hope-filled words Peter speaks to the man at the gate called Beautiful? How do those words take him beyond his inability to walk to walking, leaping, and praising God?

How does this lame man encounter the love of Jesus?

How can miracles open doors to share the love of Jesus with others?

What makes Philip leave one place to go to another place with very little information so powerful?

In what way does Philip cooperate with God's command?

Which one of the pivot points speaks to you the most? How and in what way?

What is one thing you are going to take away from this lesson?

Epilogue

STANDING ON THE ROCK OF HOPE: JESUS

⌘

"And this hope will not lead to disappointment. For we know how dearly God loves us, because he has given us the Holy Spirit to fill our hearts with his love" (Romans 5:5, NLT).

Much of this book has been about gaining hope or having our hope renewed in the midst of disappointments, setbacks, and uncertainty. How do we stand as overcomers when everything around us is so unsettling, and we feel like we have lost our hope for the present and the future? The enemy is going to speak lies to us to keep us defeated, doubting, and distressed. He will say things like: "*You are a hopeless case*" or "*You deserve what you are presently experiencing*." A person may even say to you, "*Don't get* your *hopes up*." Friend, no one is a hopeless case; we must get our hopes up! Jesus is our hope, and He will never disappoint us, let us down, or ever forsake us (Hebrews 13:6).

Jeremiah battles this sense of hopelessness in Lamentations.

> I tell myself, "I am finished! I can't count on the Lord to do anything for me." Just thinking of my troubles and my lonely wandering makes me miserable. That's

> all I ever think about, and I am depressed. **Then I remember something that fills me with hope.** The Lord's kindness never fails! If he had not been merciful, we would have been destroyed. The Lord can always be trusted to show mercy each morning. Deep in my heart I say, "The Lord is all I need; I can depend on him!" The Lord is kind to everyone who trusts and obeys him. It is good to wait patiently for the Lord to save us (Lamentations 3:18-26, CEV, emphasis added).

What truths can we draw from this passage of Scripture? We find this person has lost all hope and feels like he is a hopeless case, and the future looks bleak. He says, "I tell myself, 'I am finished! I can't count on the Lord to do anything for me'" (Lamentations 3:16, CEV). This person is depressed, lonely, and feeling separated from others, from life, and from the Lord when he says: "Just thinking of my troubles and my lonely wandering makes me miserable. That's all I ever think about, and I am depressed" (vs.19-20, CEV). You get the feeling all hope of having joy again is gone; all hope of experiencing God's promises is gone, and the sorrow he is feeling is so deep he feels he will never get over it or beyond it.

Then, something happens, and the seed of hope, promise, blessing, and provision has been sown. He begins to remember the faithfulness of God: "Then I remember something that fills me with hope. The Lord's kindness never fails! If he had not been merciful, we would have been destroyed" (vs. 21-22, CEV). The truth is the Lord will never fail us, nor let us go; He has us in the palm of His hand and will never loosen His grip on our lives. This writer not only speaks of renewed hope, but he also speaks about a new beginning as he remembers "the Lord can always be trusted to show mercy each morning" (Lamentations 3:23, CEV). The new beginning starts when we cease looking inward and begin to look outward: "Deep in my heart I say, 'The Lord is all I need; I can depend on him!'" (v. 24, CEV). It is not our faithfulness that keeps us when we feel like we have blown it and feel depleted in our strength. It is God's faithfulness that we can rely on as we place our dilemma upon Him and cast all our cares on Him because He cares for us (1 Peter 5:7).

Rediscovering Your H.O.P.E.

Let's look at H.O.P.E. as an acronym to aid us in finding our hope once again. **First** of all, the **Helper**, the Holy Spirit, brings comfort and imparts strength in the midst of our weakness. The Lord says to us, "'My power works best in weakness.'" (2 Corinthians 12:9a, NLT). Paul's response to that statement is: "So now I am glad to boast about my weaknesses, so that the power of Christ can work through me" (2 Corinthians 12:9b, NLT). There is power in our declarations. If we begin to declare the Word of God and His promises, it renews our minds to think differently and to believe differently.

One of the first things we can do to renew hope and courage is to begin declaring the Word of God over our lives, our circumstances, our setbacks, and our disappointments. The Bible teaches us, "That we through the perseverance and comfort of the Scriptures might have hope" (Romans 15:5). Talk to the Lord; He's our friend and confidante; He knows us better than we know ourselves. He sees us as we truly are, and He loves us more than anyone else in the world. Read the Bible and see that God wins—therefore we win! Jesus has come to bring us hope; focus on our hope for tomorrow.

Second, Christ has made us **overcomers** because He lives in us. The apostle Paul writes, "Yet in all these things we are more than conquerors through Him who loved us" (Romans 8:37). John, in his Epistle, observes, "He who is in you is greater that he who is in the world" (1 John 4:4). Jesus has overcome the devil, men, the world, and every other obstacle that He faced. Therefore, if the Overcomer lives in us, that makes us overcomers.

Jesus declares of Himself:

> "The Spirit of the Lord is upon Me (the Messiah), because He has anointed Me to preach the good news to the poor. He has sent Me to announce release (pardon, forgiveness) to the captives, and recovery of sight to the blind, to set free those who are oppressed (downtrodden, bruised, crushed by tragedy)" (Luke 4:18, AMP).

The word "oppression" means *worried, troubled, overloaded, burdened, depressed, and distressed.* Jesus has come to meet us where we are and take us to where we cannot go on our own.

We all have experienced these things to some degree or another, but Jesus said He comes to lift the burden, the oppression, and the depression so that we can have an abundant life. It means we begin to focus our eyes on Jesus and not so much on what we are going through. We begin by declaring, "If God is for us, who can be against us?" (Romans 8:31b). God is not finished with us; therefore, we have hope. God has a plan and a future for us, and we must choose to embrace His plan for our lives (Jeremiah 29:11). No matter how bad you have it, there is always someone who has it worse than you do. It helps to stop thinking about "ME" and develop the habit of looking outward to others. The question for us all to consider is: "*What can I do to make it better for someone else today?*"

We ask the Lord to renew our mind—to transform us so that we think differently, believe differently, and talk differently. Sometimes we have to get rid of our stinking thinking and believe the best is yet to come. Our heavenly Father is the One who lifts our heads above the storm: "But you, God, shield me on all sides; You ground my feet, You lift my head high" (Psalm 3:3, MSG). The hope we have in the Lord changes the direction of our attention from looking around at the storm to looking to Him and setting our focus on the God of all hope (2 Corinthians 1:3). This thing will surely pass. Sometimes things happen, and we feel like it's the end of the world, but it's NOT! If you take a step today, tomorrow will be different. His mercy is new every morning! He orders our steps. If you feel like you're losing it, let go of it and let God have control. Don't hesitate to ask for help; if you're feeling desperate, reach out to a Christian leader or counselor. The most important thing is to never ever quit.

> Hope comes when you don't quit. The problem with quitting is that it steals your hope. Quitting and giving up your hope only hands it over to the enemy. Endure with patience so that the manifestation of hope becomes a testimony of faith.[12]
>
> —Rabbi Curt Landry
> Founder Curt Landry Ministries

Third, He gives **peace** to the weary that brings a calm assurance of His empowering grace. Jesus said, "These things I have spoken to you, that in Me you may have peace. In the world you will have tribulation; but be of good cheer, I have overcome the world" (John 16:33). God's deep abiding peace is not fleeting as if it is here today and gone tomorrow. Our Lord blesses us with the eternal peace of God that keeps us and assures us that He has not left us at any time (Psalm 29:11). When we begin to shift our focus from ourselves and place our attention on the Lord, He will keep us in perfect peace (Isaiah 26:3) which is the manifestation of the kingdom of God (Romans 14:17). Our declaration should be: *the kingdom of God is within me, and I enjoy His peace because of His presence in me.* The peace we can experience is when we confess our sin to the Lord and ask His forgiveness for taking our eyes off of Him. Our response is to ask for forgiveness from the Lord and others and give forgiveness when needed. How do you keep hope alive?

> Make a commitment to take the seed of hope within your heart and raise it up in the protection of God's Word. Water it daily with devotion. Wrap it in prayer and ask the Holy Spirit to place ministering

> angels around you to guard and protect it. Ask the Lord for the impartation of wisdom and daily revelation of how to maintain the hope you've been given. [13]
>
> —Rabbi Curt Landry
> Founder Curt Landry Ministries

Finally, we have **entrance** into His presence with thanksgiving, as we enter His rest and as we enter into the joy of the Lord. In His presence, we can walk in fullness of joy (Psalm 16:11).

The Lord restores and renews our mind and gives us a new perspective from which to see life, others, the Lord, and ourselves. We declare that the Lord is the God of hope and the Restorer of our joy: "Now may the God of hope fill you with all joy and peace believing, that you may abound in hope by the power of the Holy Spirit" (Romans 15:13). What a powerful verse that through the Holy Spirit He fills us with hope again.

As a Christian, you are a vital part of God's plan. He has a work to do in you and through you. You are important and necessary because of the divine purpose He has for your life! You are God's hands, feet, and mouth to the world. Keep your hope in the resurrection of Jesus Christ, and you will continue to go beyond any failure, disappointment, and adversity in this life.

Let's Pray:

Father, to all who are weary, to all who have lost hope, and to all who have experienced setbacks and delays we say: "Come like a mighty river that refreshes and renews." Father, we need a fresh baptism of Your love that tells us that we are Your sons and daughters who are loved deeply, affectionately cared for, and of infinite value. Father, some of us need a new beginning—a fresh start. We ask that You would be that place of new beginnings through the fire of Your Spirit that infuses us with hope and fills us with confidence to begin again. Some of us need a complete overhaul of our lives, and for those, Father, begin deep within our hearts to know You and to experience You as we have never before. Set our hearts ablaze with Your love and with Your empowering grace. Father, we declare that today is a day of new beginnings and a place where our hearts are fueled with the power of Your Spirit. Amen.

Blessing in Christ,
Pastor Ray

ABOUT THE AUTHOR

⌘

RAY PETTY has served in pastoral ministry for over 37 years. He has pioneered and pastored churches, taught in Bible schools, directed Christian education, and organized life-changing small groups across the Southeast United States. Pastor Ray has been personally impacted by small group ministry and focuses on this solid way to develop disciples, grow leaders, and multiply the church. Ray is the author of ***Journey in Discipleship Study Guide***, ***Going Beyond***, and ***Teach Us to Pray Study Guide***. Upcoming study guide releases include ***A New Creation*** and ***A Kingdom of Power and Glory***. He received his Masters of Divinity from Asbury Theological Seminary and his bachelor's degree from Oral Roberts University. Ray is a husband, father, and grandfather; he lives in Tennessee with his wife, Alice.

FOOTNOTES

1 Chuck Pierce, ***Time To Defeat The Devil***, (Lake Mary, FL: Charisma House, 2011), Electronic Device, Loc 4417.

2 R. T. Kendal, ***These Are the Days of Elijah***, (Minneapolis, MI: Chosen), p65 Electronic Device.

3 F. B. Meyer, ***Elijah: And The Secret Of His Power***, (Fort Washington, PA: CLC Publications, Electronic Device, p9.

4 Bill Johnson, ***Defining Moments***, (Kensington, PA: Whitaker House, 2016), Electronic Device, loc 4818.

5 Bill Johnson, ***Face to Face with God***, (Lake Mary, FL: Charisma House, 2007), p47.

6 Frank Damazio, ***From Barrenness to Fruitfulness***, (Ventura, CA: Regal Books, 1998) p72.

7 Ibid. p65

8 Wayne Corderio, and Robert Lewis, Culture Shift, (San Francisco, CA: Publisher Jossey-Bass, 2005), p88.

9 C. Peter Wagner, ***The Book of Acts: A Commentary*** (Minneapolis, MN: Chosen Books, 1994), p201.

10 Bill Johnson, ***Defining Moments***, Electric Device, Loc 4598.

11 George Barna, ***Growing True Disciples***, (WaterBrook Press: Random House, New York, NY, 2001), p62.

12 Curt Landry, "What Do You Do When You've Lost Hope," The Elijah List (December 21, 2018): http://http://www.elijahlist.com/words/display_word.html?ID=21321.

13 Ibid.

BIBLIOGRAPHY

Barna, George. ***Growing True Disciples***, WaterBrook Press: Random House, New York, NY, 2001.

Corderio, Wayne, and Lewis, Robert. ***Culture Shift***, San Francisco, CA: Published by Jossey-Bass, 2005.

Damazio, Frank. ***From Barrenness to Fruitfulness***, Ventura, CA: Regal Books, 1998.

Johnson, Bill. ***Face to Face with Go***d, Lake Mary, FL: Charisma House, 2007.

Johnson, Bill. ***Defining Moments***, New Kensington, PA: Whitaker House, 2016.

Kendal, R. T. ***These Are the Days of Elijah***, (Minneapolis, MI: Chosen, 2013), p65.

Meyer, F. B. "***Beside the Drying Brook***," Sermon, Promoting Genuine Biblical Revival PDF: 2002-2018 SermonIndex.Net.

Pierce, Chuck. ***Time To Defeat The Devil***, Lake Mary, FL: Charisma House, 2011.

Wagner, C. Peter. ***The Book of Acts: A Commentary***, Minneapolis, Minnesota: Chosen Books, 1994.

Parsons Publishing House

Your Voice Your World ™

GOING BEYOND—From Your Path of Disappointment to God's Overcoming Love

Have you ever experienced setbacks, failures, or disappointments at some level in your life? Most people have. Come with me to a place called Beyond—beyond our failures, beyond our self-doubts, beyond our disappointments, and beyond our fears. It is time to renew your faith to trust in God's unceasing love and endless mercy to take the next step in your walk with Him. Ray Petty explores Going Beyond:

- PRESS into God's best—His goodness and greatness.
- BELIEVE that God takes the worst & turns it to our best.
- EXPERIENCE more than we can ask, think, believe, or imagine.
- WATCH God work all things together for our good and His glory.

Let this book take you to a place called "Beyond" to experience the extravagance of God's love and His ability to do in us and through what we cannot do on our own. For individual or group study.2

ISBN: 9781602731059 • 202 pages • 5.5x8.5 in • $12.95 USD

JOURNEY IN DISCIPLESHIP STUDY GUIDE

This powerful stand-alone study guide by Ray Petty, issues a call to become a relevant follower of Christ as an agent of change in your world. Through these 16 Bible lessons, you will gain a foundation for your service and a practical road-map into becoming more like Jesus Christ. This is for use in your individual or group study to find answers about:

- Revealing God's explosive power in YOUR life
- Finding YOUR place in Christian community
- Wielding God's Word for YOUR victorious living
- Functioning in YOUR supernatural wholeness

ISBN: 9781602730939 • 202 pages • 5.5x8.5 in • $10.95 USD

Parsons Publishing House
Your Voice Your World™

TEACH US TO PRAY STUDY GUIDE

Jesus did not teach His disciples how to preach, teach, or how to grow a church; however, Jesus did teach them how to pray. This 13-lesson study guide for individual or group study includes practical exercises teaches us how mature Christians move from asking the Father to release His Kingdom to declaring the promises of God over ourselves, our family, in our community, and over our nation.

ISBN: 9781602731080 • 5.5x8.5 in

AVAILABLE AT YOUR LOCAL BOOKSTORE, AMAZON, OR OTHER RETAIL OUTLETS.

Contact Information

For speaking engagements or special book orders, contact:

Pastor Ray Petty
RayPetty@hotmail.com